Warwick Studies in Industrial Relations

Disputes Procedure in Action

Warwick Studies in Industrial Relations

General Editors: George Bain, Hugh Clegg, Allan Flanders

Disputes Procedure in Action, R. Hyman
Race and Industrial Conflict, M. Rimmer
The London Docks since Devlin, M. Mellish

Disputes Procedure in Action

A Study of the Engineering Industry Disputes Procedure in Coventry

Richard Hyman

Lecturer in Industrial Relations, University of Warwick and Associate Fellow, Social Science Research Council Industrial Relations Research Unit

H·E·B

HEINEMANN EDUCATIONAL BOOKS
LONDON

Heinemann Educational Books Ltd

LONDON EDINBURGH MELBOURNE TORONTO
SINGAPORE JOHANNESBURG AUCKLAND
IBADAN HONG KONG NAIROBI NEW DELHI
KUALA LUMPUR

ISBN 0 435 85320 1

First published 1972

Published by
Heinemann Educational Books Ltd
48 Charles Street, London W1X 8AH
Printed in Great Britain by
Willmer Brothers Limited, Birkenhead

Editors' Foreword

Warwick University's first undergraduates were admitted in 1965. The teaching of industrial relations began a year later, and in 1967 a one-year graduate course leading to an M.A. in Industrial Relations was introduced. At about the same time a grant from the Clarkson Trustees allowed a beginning to be made on a research project concerned with several aspects of industrial relations in selected Coventry plants.

In 1970 the Social Science Research Council established three Research Units, one of them being the Industrial Relations Research Unit at Warwick. The Unit took over the Coventry project and developed others, including studies of union growth, union organisation, occupational labour markets, coloured immigrants in industry, ideologies of 'fairness' in industrial relations and the effects of the Industrial Relations Act.

This monograph series is intended to form the main vehicle for the publication of the results of the Unit's projects, of the research carried out by staff teaching industrial relations in the University, and, where it merits publication, of the work of graduate students. Some of these results will, of course, be published as articles, and some in the end may constitute full-scale volumes. But the monograph is the most apt form for much of our work. Industrial relations research is concerned with assembling and analysing evidence much of which cannot be succinctly summarised in tables and graphs, so that an adequate presentation of findings can easily take too much space for an article. On the other hand, even with a major project which will in the end lead to one or more books, there is often an advantage in publishing interim results as monographs. This is particularly true where the project deals, as do several of the industrial relations studies at Warwick, with problems of current interest for which employers, trade unionists and governments are anxiously seeking solutions.

Dr. Hyman's study of the working of the national Engineering Disputes Procedure in Coventry, which is one of the products of the Coventry project, is an appropriate example of research into such a problem. In December 1971 the national engineering procedure was terminated, repeated attempts at revision having foundered on the rock of what is known as the *status quo* clause. For the time being engineering will have to make do with informal *ad hoc* local arrangements in dealing with disputes that cannot be settled within the plant, but the search for a new agreed procedure will continue. The Donovan Commission, the Industrial Relations Act and the government's draft Code of Industrial Relations Practice all emphasize the importance of improving disputes procedures in British industry. Dr. Hyman's findings concerning the strength and weaknesses of the old engineering procedure as it worked in Coventry, the behaviour of the participants, the success of procedure in handling different types of disputes and the need for flexibility, hold interest for everyone concerned with the reform of disputes procedures.

GEORGE BAIN
HUGH CLEGG
ALLAN FLANDERS

Contents

Author's Preface

None of the research discussed in this paper would have been possible without the extensive co-operation of the Coventry and District Engineering Employers' Association. My thanks are due to the staff of the Association, and also to the many trade union officials and managers who gave their assistance. In addition I would like to thank those colleagues at Warwick who offered advice and criticism on earlier drafts of this monograph.

RICHARD HYMAN

List of Tables

List of Abbreviations

ACTSS	Association of Clerical, Technical and Supervisory Staffs
AEF	Amalgamated Union of Engineering and Foundry Workers
ASPD	Amalgamated Society of Painters and Decorators
ASSET	Association of Supervisory Staffs, Executives and Technicians
ASTMS	Association of Scientific, Technical and Managerial Staffs
ASW	Amalgamated Society of Woodworkers
ASWM	Amalgamated Society of Woodworking Machinists
AUBTW	Amalgamated Union of Building Trade Workers
AUFW	Amalgamated Union of Foundry Workers
BMSMW	Birmingham and Midland Sheet Metal Workers' Society
CAWU	Clerical and Administrative Workers' Union
CC	Central Conference
DATA	Draughtsmen's and Allied Technicians' Association
EEF	Engineering Employers' Federation
ETU	Electrical Trades Union
FTA	Failure to agree
GMWU	General and Municipal Workers' Union
IRA	Industrial Relations Act
JWC	Joint Works Committee
LC	Local Conference
NACSS	National Association of Clerical and Supervisory Staffs
NSMM	National Society of Metal Mechanics
NUSMWC	National Union of Sheet Metal Workers and Coppersmiths
NUVB	National Union of Vehicle Builders
TGWU	Transport and General Workers' Union
UPA	United Patternmakers' Association
WC	Works Conference

Introduction

The disputes procedure in British engineering is the oldest in any major national industry, and despite some adjustments its basic features remain those devised by the federated employers in 1898. The virtual uniqueness of many of its characteristics—viewed by some commentators as anachronistic—explains in part why engineering procedure has long been 'the most criticized of all such agreements in the country'.[1] The persistence of this traditional system owes much to the enthusiastic commitment of the employers' organization, which has itself altered little in structure since the 1890s, remaining a national federation of district associations exercising considerable local autonomy.

But the longevity of procedure must be attributed in part to the engineering trade unions. Its origins in two national lock-outs have ensured for procedure the formal hostility of the unions; yet they remained willing to operate within its framework for a quarter of a century in which the balance of power had shifted significantly. Indeed, the national discussions on procedural reform which commenced in 1969 were initiated by the Engineering Employers' Federation (EEF); and this initiative owed much to forthright criticisms recorded by such *outside* observers as the Royal Commission on Trade Unions and Employers' Associations and the National Board for Prices and Incomes.

At the time of writing (mid 1971) the future of the engineering procedure is uncertain. By the date of publication, some at least of the trade unions may have withdrawn from the national procedure agreement; or a radically revised version may have been agreed. Nevertheless, this study aspires to be of more than historical interest. An account of how particular issues become the subject of procedural discussions, and the manner in which they are handled, is of continuing relevance; so is a discussion of such fundamental questions as why employers and unions choose to regulate their relationships through such mechanisms. In short, many of the factors involved concern far broader elements of the industrial relations context than the form of procedure itself. For this reason, the present tense is used throughout.

The research is based on the operation of procedure in the area of the Coventry and District Engineering Employers' Association. The two main sources of data are an analysis of the records of procedural conferences over a period of several years; and a detailed examination of thirty-three references which entered Works Conference during a five-week period in 1970. The latter involved attendance at many of the conferences, and discussions with representatives of managements, trade unions, and the Employers' Association.

Engineering is an extremely heterogeneous industry (or complex of industries) and displays considerable geographical variation. Differences in technology and company structure, in the quality and personality of management and union officials, in Employers' Association policy, and in local bargaining traditions, combine to render industrial relations in each district to some extent unique. Yet the operation of a disputes procedure also involves problems common to every local context. For this reason, the research is perhaps of more than local interest.

The structure and findings of this study may be briefly summarized. Chapter I explains the procedural provisions that cover various categories of employees in engineering, and describes how the external procedure, with its three-stage system of conferences, operates in Coventry.

In Chapter II, recent trends in the use of procedure are considered. The increase in the procedural workload since the end of the 1950s has often been noted. In Coventry, the number of conferences has increased at almost double the national rate. However, this explosive growth both locally and nationally appears to have moderated and perhaps halted in the late 1960s.

Chapter III discusses the role of the trade unions in initiating references in procedure. Analysis of Coventry references shows the predominance of the two largest organizations, the AEF and the TGWU. While smaller manual unions are involved in references roughly in proportion to the size of their membership, most of these rarely initiate references independently, but rather appear primarily in the minority of multi-union references. To some extent, this would seem to reflect union policy.

In Chapter IV, the role of the companies is examined. Local statistics fail to reveal the disproportionate involvement of the largest firms, and of car-manufacturing establishments, which previous national research has indicated. But great variation occurs in the use of procedure by firms facing apparently similar problems and conditions, and by individual firms in different years. One relevant factor is the variation which can exist in *willingness* to use procedure in different companies and at different times.

An attempt is made in Chapter V to outline a theoretical framework in order to interpret the trends and variations which exist in the use of engineering procedure. The disputes procedure is often viewed as a form of judicial process; in fact it is best conceived as a type of bargaining. More specifically, engineering procedure as it operates in Coventry typically involves the kind of issue bargaining in which gain by one side is at the expense of the other. Less clear-cut problems which can be resolved to the mutual advantage of both parties do not seem suited to the structure of engineering procedure, and are far more likely to be dealt with informally. In this way, the questions arising domestically are to an important extent pre-selected before they enter external procedure.

The readiness of unions to make increasing use of procedure cannot be explained simply by their formal obligations under the national agreement—for it has always been open to them to withdraw from this agreement. In fact, with a high proportion of references—particularly those involving straightforward wage claims—unions do seem able to achieve some improvement on the company's domestic offer. Even where no such concession is forthcoming, union officials may well feel that the use of procedure prevents the involvement of members in more vigorous action which might prove no more effective.

The reasons why companies make concessions in procedure which are not forthcoming domestically are often complex. There is little evidence to justify the charge of deliberate delaying tactics by managements, though managerial indecision does appear at times to force questions into procedure which might reasonably be involved domestically. At times, reference to external procedure may be an element in a conflict *within* management regarding the handling of a union claim. And in some companies, the executive with authority to concede a particular demand may become involved in negotiations only after reference to external procedure.

The dynamics of the bargaining process itself also inhibit domestic settlement of some questions. A firm stand in domestic discussions is one way in which either side may try to impress the other with its determination in a particular case. More generally, experience at a particular company may persuade each side that the other will begin serious negotiation only when discussions have reached a certain stage. It is easy to see that such expectations can become self-validating and self-perpetuating. Without a deliberate effort by both sides to prevent this, an 'escalation of the level of settlement' can easily occur spontaneously and unintentionally.

There are of course more positive reasons for both sides

to use external procedure. One reason why the formal conference can assist the bargaining process would seem to be that it creates a situation which all concerned recognize as to some extent artificial. The ritual which surrounds a conference emphasizes the fact that all are performing roles. As a result, a hostile interchange which occurs, say, between Union and Association representatives will not be taken personally; officials who have in effect to live with each other can divorce what they do and say on behalf of their organizations from their relationship as individuals. The contrived atmosphere of procedure also makes it easier for negotiators to commit themselves to positions and then alter or abandon these without loss of face.

Procedure can in some circumstances be of great value simply as a mechanism for introducing outside negotiators within an industry strongly committed to domestic autonomy. In addition to any personal skills they may contribute, outside professionals bring with them a network of conventions and shared understandings which develop naturally in the course of regular interaction, and which can be particularly important in facilitating the bargaining process.

The narrow terms of reference common in engineering procedure can also assist the settlement of questions arising, since the area of dispute is so closely delineated; questions of principle may even be transformed into issues which admit more readily of compromise. Yet this same factor can give rise to a more general problem; how both sides (but particularly management) should treat references which enter external procedure. Refusal to modify the domestic position invites the charge of inflexibility, of destroying the whole point of procedure; concessions invite further references to procedure and the inhibition of domestic settlement. Precisely because most references are straightforward bargaining issues rather than questions of obvious principle, it has little meaning to say that each case should be judged on its merits. The negotiators must therefore devote much of their attention, implicitly at least, to considering the balance of forces in the case in question and the implication of the various possible outcomes for future issues.

This point has relevance for the interpretation of the significance of unconstitutional strikes and other forms of sanctions. Customarily these are viewed as a breakdown in the collective bargaining relationship. Employers often attribute such action to a failure of communication within trade unions; trade unions, to provocative actions or inadequate consultation by employers. Both interpretations ignore the possibility that the use of sanctions may be intimately related to collective bargaining as such. The nature of contemporary industrial relations in engineering ensures that most references to procedure are merely sectional pay claims which happen not to have been resolved domestically. Whatever the perspicacity and bargaining skill of the external negotiators, the eventual settlement is normally shaped largely by the relative strength of the domestic protagonists and the assessment each makes of the other's determination. Sanctions applied by the party seeking substantive change may provide a show of strength or an indication of determination and thus function as an integral part of the bargaining process.

If—as would seem to be the case—the outside organizations of both workers and employers seek to encourage the domestic resolution of disputes, the initiating party is in effect encouraged to assist the process by applying sanctions before, or instead of, referring a deadlocked claim to external procedure. This is particularly the case where it seems unlikely that any concession will otherwise be forthcoming in external procedure; and where an issue is of a perishable nature (i.e., where it must be resolved quickly if at all—as with a disputed dismissal). This fact would seem to help explain the somewhat ambivalent attitudes which those involved in engineering procedure take towards unconstitutional action.

Engineering procedure has been subject to a number of criticisms; in particular, it has commonly been charged with excessive delay, with a bias towards management, and with failing to resolve positively enough of the questions referred to it. These allegations are considered in Chapter VI.

The Coventry references studied involved an average delay of a little less than a month between Works and Local Conference, and about two months between Local and Central; local cases were thus processed somewhat faster than those references covered by a national study for the year 1959. While the delays which did occur do not seem attributable to deliberate tactics by companies, neither does any shortage of union officers seem primarily responsible. Important contributory factors are the heavy engagements of *all* the parties involved; the considerable built-in delay at the Central Conference stage; and the delay inherent in the bargaining process itself.

Engineering procedure is notable for its device of 'employer conciliation'. In Coventry the mechanism of the employers' panel has lost much of its formality, and while it may still be of significant value in some cases, it seems unlikely that these are more than a small minority. The Employers' Association official who must act both as Chairman and as spokesman for one protagonist is inevitably involved in conflict of roles; while this is normally handled skilfully, it can give rise to difficulties. The controversial 'managerial functions' clause, as it operates in Coventry, appears in practice as only a minor handicap to trade unionism; companies are in most circumstances prepared to apply procedure with a flexibility which approximates to the operation of *status quo*. Yet this is not universally the case; and such flexibility occurs precisely in the context of worker ability and readiness to apply extra-constitutional sanctions.

The effectiveness of a disputes procedure is normally assessed on the basis of its 'disposal rates'. In Coventry, in recent years, Works Conference appears less effective than the national average; Local, about the same; while Central Conferences on local claims have achieved a slightly higher than average disposal rate. But these rates fluctuate considerably from year to year. Moreover, a high proportion of conferences—particularly at Central level—do not result in any clear and positive outcome *within* procedure: about half the references reaching Works Conference in Coventry are instead resolved in informal or domestic discussions.

It would seem that engineering procedure in this district does achieve a considerable degree of effectiveness, but this is to a large extent because the operation of the formal system of conferences is intermeshed with far more flexible and informal processes of dispute handling. It is precisely because the formal prescriptions of procedure are *not* rigidly enforced that the system seems relatively acceptable to the parties involved.

It appears probable that any revised procedure would require a continuation of these informal mechanisms, to provide a flexible link between workplace systems of industrial relations based to a large extent on custom and practice, and the external institutions of the industry. Indeed, a streamlining of the procedure may well necessitate further elaboration of informal channels of negotiation. It is finally suggested that any attempt to impose on British industrial relations a rigid and legalistic framework—in which the parties' mutual expectations and shared understandings would, for a time at least, be disrupted—could well jeopardize the whole basis of informal relationships which underlie the sensitive process of successful dispute resolution.

REFERENCES

1. A. I. Marsh, *Industrial Relations in Engineering*, Pergamon, 1965, p. 117

I

The Nature of Engineering Procedure

The procedure relating to manual workers, as it operates at the time of the study, is based on the national agreement which followed the lock-out of 1922, with the incorporation of certain minor amendments agreed in 1955. A statement of general principles, and of the circumstances in which procedure is to apply, is followed by the Provisions for Avoiding Disputes:

(a) When a question arises, an endeavour shall be made by the Management and the workman directly concerned to settle the same in the works or at the place where the question has arisen. Failing settlement deputations of workmen who may be accompanied by their Organiser (in which event a representative of the Employers' Association shall also be present) shall be received by the Employers by appointment without unreasonable delay for the mutual discussion of any question in the settlement of which both parties are directly concerned. In the event of no settlement being arrived at it shall be competent for either party to bring the question before a Local Conference to be held between the Local Association and the local representative of the Society.

(b) In the event of either party desiring to raise any question a Local Conference for this purpose may be arranged by application to the Secretary of the Local Association or to the local representative of the Society.

(c) Local Conferences shall be held within seven working days, unless otherwise mutually agreed upon, from the receipt of the application by the Secretary of the Local Association or the local representative of the Society.

(d) Failing settlement at a Local Conference of any question brought before it, it shall be competent for either party to refer the matter to a Central Conference which, if thought desirable, may make a joint recommendation to the constituent bodies.

(e) Central Conference shall be held on the second Friday of each month at which questions referred to Central Conference prior to fourteen days of that date shall be taken.

(f) Until the procedure provided above has been carried through, there shall be no stoppage of work either of a partial or a general character.

These provisions are based, with only minor verbal alterations on the York Memorandum of 1914; and their principles derive from the earlier national agreements of 1898 and 1907.

The first clause, in its reference to domestic negotiations, reflects the pre-First World War situation when collective bargaining on the shop floor was undeveloped and the deputation of workmen a typical mechanism. Modern realities receive more explicit (though still brief) acknowledgement elsewhere in the agreement, where some of the functions of shop stewards are specified. The bridge between internal and external procedure—the Works Conference—is nowhere mentioned by name, though the title became accepted by both parties soon after procedure was first instituted.

Separate procedural arrangements cover apprentices, boys and youths, and non-manual workers. For the former category these were agreed in 1937. One obvious difference from the York Memorandum is the absence of a formal Central Conference; but a 'National Conference' of Federation and union officials is intended to fulfil a similar function. In the district studied, the earlier stages of procedure appeared in their practical operation to be identical to those for adult workers.

Arrangements for staff employees are based on separate agreements reached at various dates between the EEF and individual unions. While based in broad outline on the procedure for manual workers, each of these agreements displays some differences in detail; in general, the status of staff unions within procedure is somewhat more restricted. The Federation has traditionally been concerned to segregate the processing of manual and staff issues, one obvious feature of this separate treatment is that while procedure for manual workers has traditionally ended at York, staff Central Conferences are held in London. The procedure agreements with staff unions appear to allow some scope for local variation in operation; practice in the Coventry district suggests that the Employers' Association is willing to accord virtual parity of treatment with the manual unions.

The Federation has shown particular sensitivity in respect of questions arising in connection with supervisory staff. In consequence, the agreement signed in 1944 with the Association of Supervisory Staffs, Executives and Technicians (ASSET)—now Division 1 of the Association of Scientific, Technical and Managerial Staffs (ASTMS) —is 'unlike any other procedure agreement in the engineering industry'.[1] Recognition was for many years resisted by the EEF, and was conceded only as a result of the embarrassment caused by the Association's skilful use of the wartime arbitration machinery. The price of recognition for ASSET was however a procedure extremely restricted in scope. National negotiations as such are not authorized; and access to procedure is confined to establishments in which the Association has majority membership in the grade concerned (all other unions can refer questions to procedure irrespective of the proportion of workers represented). Until amended in 1966, the procedure agreement made no reference to a system of formal conferences; though in the district studied, Works and Local Conferences were in fact held and referred to as such. The latter do not, however, possess the formality customary with references involving other unions. It would appear that the rigidity or flexibility with which the agreement is applied can vary markedly between districts.[2]

The Operation of Procedure

The Works Conference, as its title implies, is held at the establishment at which a reference arises. On application by the trade union or company concerned, the Employers' Association arranges a date convenient for all parties. At the time agreed, or shortly beforehand, each 'outside' representative arrives and takes part in preliminary briefing discussions: the union official with his shop stewards, the Association representative with members of management. Usually this requires about half an hour, though a highly complex reference may necessitate longer pre-conference discussion.

At the conference proper, each side faces the other across the table. There are usually three or four representatives on each side; but in the cases studied there were occasionally as many as seven management and ten trade-union representatives. To some extent, the size of a conference may indicate its importance. On the management side, a small matter may require the presence of a departmental supervisor and the personnel or industrial relations officer; more weighty cases may bring in the works manager, a more senior industrial relations executive, and such staff functionaries as the industrial engineer. On the union side, references involving several departments may require representatives from each as well as a senior steward; multi-union cases often involve a duplication of both lay and full-time representation.

The conference is opened by the Chairman, who is always an employer representative, and in Coventry almost invariably the Association official. After stating the terms of reference he invites the union official to present his case (or, with an 'employer's reference', the Chairman himself makes the opening submission). This opening statement is commonly a fairly detailed argument lasting some five or ten minutes—though this will vary according to the complexity of the reference and the loquacity of the official. A few brief exchanges may be necessary to clarify certain points; it is then normal for the company side to adjourn in order to discuss the union's case.[3] Occasionally the company may reply without an adjournment, having fully anticipated the union's case. But this is rare; for even if the union's arguments are predictable, to reply without an adjournment may give the impression that they have not been taken seriously.

In the adjournment (which in the cases studied could last anywhere between ten minutes and an hour) the company may merely agree to reaffirm its previous position; or the Employers' Association official, or a member of management not previously involved in the case, may suggest a different response; or a new perspective introduced by the union in its submission may require consideration.

On resumption of the conference, the company reply is stated by the Chairman. If this represents no change from the position in domestic discussions, the union normally registers failure to agree after little further argument.[4] If some concession is offered, or is implicit in the reply, several exchanges usually occur during which the union official seeks to clarify the management offer and probe the possibility of further movement. He in turn then normally requests an adjournment in order to discuss with his steward the significance of the reply, the likelihood of further concessions, and the probable reaction of the shop floor. When the conference again resumes, the official indicates whether or not the company position is favourably received; further discussion then ensues. In principle, further cycles of adjournment and resumption are possible. But in all conferences attended, after at most two adjournments a conclusion was reached; either (infrequently) a hard and fast agreement, or, more commonly, a decision to adjourn or refer back the reference in the hope of settlement; or else failure to agree.

The process of discussion at Works Conference tends normally to approximate to a dialogue. On the union side, it would be an exaggeration to suggest that domestic representatives never speak unless asked to; but there appears to be an informal convention that they normally intervene only to emphasize a point made by the full-time official, or to provide information on an issue of fact. On the company side, interventions by members of management are more frequent, but the Chairman normally plays the dominant role.

While the basic structure of the Local Conference is very similar, the occasion is one of greater formality—the tone being set by the imposing surroundings of the Employers' Association conference room. The characteristic features of this stage of procedure have been summarized as follows by the EEF:

> Although . . . the detailed arrangements vary in different parts of the country, the universal principle is that the question referred is discussed between the district officials of the union concerned and a committee composed of representative engineering employers from the same association area. These employers are not directly concerned in the case and they are supported by a senior official of the association. The company is represented at the conference by members of the management and the workpeople through their shop steward (or stewards). In addition, the proceedings as between the union(s) and the employers' committee are recorded by a shorthand writer. The essence of this stage in the procedure is that it brings new minds and wider experience to bear on the issue raised and that, particularly in those cases where no settlement is reached, the differences between the parties are further clarified and put on record, together with the supporting observations and arguments.[5]

The device of the 'employers' panel' represents a quasi-judicial institution, yet one originally designed to safeguard managerial interests. As Marsh suggests, the panel 'is convened to hear the two sides of the case as presented by the union and the firm concerned'; but it has always been a fundamental principle that it should be unable 'to negotiate away the individual employer's rights on any particular issue as he conceived them'.[6] In practice at least in the district studied—the panel has a far less central role than is suggested by the formal provisions. Local practice is for the Association to invite only two or three representatives of member firms—and not all can necessarily attend. Managers from the company involved thus often outnumber the 'external' panel. In conference proceedings, the panel can scarcely be said to 'hear' the company case in the same manner that it hears that of the union; for company representatives, Chairman and panel all meet beforehand to discuss the reference; all sit on the same side of the table; and if the panel members wish to probe or question the company case, they do so in privacy of adjournments.

The conduct of Local Conferences is obviously affected by the presence of the shorthand writer; for each side is constantly aware that its arguments may subsequently be scrutinized by the Central Conference authorities, who receive the verbatim notes of all cases referred to them. Each party must therefore ensure that its case is stated in the most comprehensive and comprehensible form possible, and that nothing is said which may weaken the case. Considerable circumspection is therefore necessary; a constraint which is hardly conducive to sensitive negotiation.[7] However, managers and officials familiar with this situation do not appear to find the constraints particularly onerous. If serious bargaining is to occur it is merely necessary for the parties to 'go off the notes'; the official transcript then simply records the cryptic comment: 'informal discussion ensued'. Informal discussion is also possible during an adjournment; occasionally the union official alone may return to the conference room, or may meet the Chairman in the corridor, in order to clarify a company proposal or to discuss a form of words for a settlement.

By tradition, Central Conferences for manual workers are held at the Royal Station Hotel, York, on the second Friday of every month. The procedure followed has been summarized by the EEF:

> The discussions are between representatives of the national executive authorities on both sides, and the company, association and local union representatives are present at York for separate consultation with their respective executives but do not take part in the formal discussions between the national representatives. A verbatim report of the formal proceedings is taken. This record, unless otherwise decided on, is private and confidential to the national bodies.
>
> Each 'court', i.e. employers' committee, consists of federated employers who have no direct interest in the company concerned

in the question at issue, and neither the chairman nor the members of the court come from the same area whence the question has been raised (e.g. an employer on the conference committee from the London Association area cannot be a member of or chair a court while it is dealing with a question arising from the London area). The constitution of the Federation provides for the appointment of the conference committee. It consists of employers of high standing in the industry who attend central conference either on a regular basis or on rota. . . .

Although central conference is the last stage in the procedure, the outcome of a case can take several different forms. The discussion in many cases leads to the evolution of lines of possible settlement, which justifies a reference back of the question for further consideration at domestic, works conference or local conference level and final settlement. Other cases are settled in central conference, but in yet other cases, the employers and union executives are not satisfied either that all the underlying facts have been brought out or that the parties concerned locally can resolve their difficulties without further assistance from the national representatives. The question may therefore be retained in the hands of central conference to allow further discussions to take place but this means that further consideration may be given to the question in central conference in the event of the parties locally being unable to resolve the matter. Occasionally a visit of inspection may be arranged to examine on the spot operations or manning practices that are in dispute. Less frequently a 'composite conference' may be agreed, i.e. a conference involving all levels on both sides—shop stewards, district and national union officers on the one side, and on the other side, the management, the local association official(s) and one or more members of the conference committee. Such conferences normally take place at the works where the issue arose and provide a special opportunity for sorting out an unsatisfactory industrial relations situation.[8]

While local representatives are excluded from the formal conference proceedings, they participate in briefing discussions with national officials on the Thursday evening and are available for consultation during conference adjournments; it would seem that the rising conference workload has increased the dependence of the central authorities on the advice and consultation of the parties directly concerned.

Staff Central Conferences are held in London, normally

on the penultimate Thursday of each month. Proceedings are in general similar to those at York.

REFERENCES

1. G. S. Bain, *The Growth of White-Collar Unionism*, Clarendon, 1970, p. 172. This work may be consulted for details of the recognition of all staff unions in engineering. The title given for ASSET in the text above is that adopted in 1946.
2. Following the formation of ASTMS in 1968, discussions have been held with a view to negotiating a single revised procedure agreement; at the time of writing, each Division of ASTMS operates its previous procedure agreement. More recently, the EEF has also discussed procedural revision with the other staff unions.
3. Adjournments emphasize the differing status within procedure of company and union. Normally at Works, and invariably at Local Conferences, the union side withdraws while the company remains in the conference room. (The rare exceptions at Works Conferences occur when the union representation is large and no adequate adjournment room is readily available).
4. As Marsh indicates (*Industrial Relations in Engineering*, p. 87), in formal records of Central Conference 'the expression "failure-to-agree" is never used'. This is not however true of the earlier stages of procedure; and even at York, this expression is used *informally* by the parties themselves.
5. Engineering Employers' Federation, *Written Evidence to the Royal Commission on Trade Unions and Employers' Associations*, paras. 168–9.
6. Marsh, op. cit., pp. 84, 116.
7. One employer has stated this constraint in an extreme form: 'you dare not open your mouth, because what everyone is concerned with is not the issue but what goes on the verbatim notes'. (Philips Industries, *Oral Evidence to the Royal Commission on Trade Unions and Employers' Associations*, q. 4198, p. 1102.)
8. *Written Evidence*, para. 173.

2

Trends in the Use of Procedure

The most obvious trend in the use of engineering procedure is the sharp increase in references since the late 1950s. To cite a recent commentary:

> Levels of procedural activity in the industry from 1898 to the present day have varied widely—although to some extent a correlation can be established between high levels of activity and the upswing of the trade cycle. However, since 1958 the trend has been inexorably upwards. Since that time total numbers of manual worker conferences have become greatly inflated, while staff worker conferences have increased by more than four and a half times. In the process 'disposal rates' at Works and Local Conferences have tended to fall and the burden on Central Conference has increased. (In recent years this seems to have been accompanied by an increase in the rate of 'failures to agree' at Central Conference and it is interesting to note that for manual workers these are now running at a higher rate than they were for most periods between the wars.)[1]

In the years between the institution of procedure and the outbreak of the First World War, Central Conference dealt on average with only some 20 cases. War, and the early years of depression, brought peaks which approached 200 cases, but the annual average fell below 50 in the early 1930s. Rearmament and the Second World War brought a new peak of about 200; but the Central Conference caseload again subsided, to below 100 in 1957. The trend in the 1960s, to nearly 600 cases at York, was wholly unprecedented. Staff Central Conferences, which reached significant numbers only in the late 1950s, experienced a similar explosive increase to a peak of 350.

Statistics showing recent trends in the conference workload and in 'disposal rates' are given in the annex to this chapter. At national level, these indicate clearly the rapid general increase in the procedural workload, the particularly sharp rise in staff references, and the 'escalation of level of settlement'.[2] What is also apparent is that this explosion in the use of procedure has subsided markedly in the late 1960s: after reaching a peak in the middle of the decade, the number of conferences at every level, for both manual workers and staff, has fluctuated erratically. These year-to-year fluctuations make it impossible to determine whether the previous expansion has come to a halt or merely decelerated.

Disposal rates nationally have fallen significantly. In some 5 per cent of manual references, procedure is exhausted without settlement, compared with 2–3 per cent in the 1950s. This trend is due not so much to an increased rate of failure to agree at York (in the late 1960s this fell to the level of the previous decade) as to lower disposal rates at the earlier stages of procedure. Staff references have shown a considerable increase in failure to agree at all levels of procedure, compared with the 1950s, together with large fluctuations from year to year.[3]

In Coventry and district, the overall number of conferences has increased at almost double the rate nationally; the proportionate increase has been particularly great at the highest levels of procedure and for staff references—where the national rate of growth has itself been highest. In most years, the proportion of local Works Conference references for manual workers reaching York is considerably higher than the national average; but a higher proportion is generally resolved *at* Central Conference (though considerable year-to-year fluctuations occur). In most years, the overall disposal rate for references entering the external procedure is below the national average. For staff workers, the proportion of Works Conference references from Coventry reaching Central Conference is in many years double the national average, though this ratio—both locally and nationally—varies erratically from year to year. Central Conference disposal rates also fluctuate, but often counteract the lower disposal of Coventry references at earlier stages in procedure. But in almost every recent year, the overall disposal rate of Coventry staff references has been below the national average—often significantly so.[4]

REFERENCES

1. A. I. Marsh and W. E. J. McCarthy, *Disputes Procedures in Britain*, Royal Commission Research Paper 2, Part 2, H.M.S.O., 1968, p. 27.
2. The phrase is taken from the Commission on Industrial Relations, *Report No.* 4, Cmnd. 4264, 1970, p. 29.
3. This may reflect the tendency of staff unions to support national claims for improvements by identical claims at plant level.
4. This may conceivably reflect managerial resistance to pace-setting claims from staff unions locally.

ANNEX

The number of hearings at each level of procedure, in Coventry and nationally, is shown below for the years 1954 to 1969; the percentage of all hearings represented by Coventry references is also given. Table I presents the number of hearings of manual workers' references; Table II, hearings of staff references (excluding those involving Division 1 of ASTMS (formerly ASSET); because of the special procedural provisions such references are normally segregated statistically by the EEF). Table III shows 'disposal rates' at each stage of procedure, nationally and locally, for manual and staff references in the years 1963–9; column 1 shows Central Conference hearings as a percentage of Works Conferences (indicating the proportion of references resolved or dropped at the earlier levels of external procedure); column 2, the percentage of Central Conferences resulting in 'failure to agree'; and column 3, the percentage of Works Conference references ending in 'failure to agree' at Central Conference.

TABLE I

Hearings, Manual Workers

	COVENTRY			NATIONAL			COVENTRY AS %		
	WC	*LC*	*CC*	*WC*	*LC*	*CC*	*WC*	*LC*	*CC*
7.54–6.55	61	8	4	1564	282	113	3·9	2·8	3·9
10.56–9.57	63	2	3	1484	320	80	4·2	0·6	3·7
11.57–10.58	79	7	3	1800	337	121	4·4	2·1	2·5
1959	77	16	8	2033	359	147	3·8	4·5	5·4
1960	92	14	10	2407	415	183	3·8	3·4	5·5
1961	66	14	8	2718	551	250	2·4	2·5	3·2
1962	80	12	8	2949	618	276	2·7	1·9	2·9
1963	94	24	15	2990	656	296	3·1	3·7	5·1
1964	181	60	23	3271	789	335	5·5	7·6	6·9
1965	257	109	42	4016	1040	434	6·4	10·5	9·7
1966	236	92	36	3854	1033	519	6·1	8·9	6·9
1967	263	81	35	4499	1071	435	5·8	7·6	8·0
1968	281	101	36	4499	1223	580	6·3	8·3	6·2
1969	308	113	66	4814	1159	555	6·4	9·7	11·9

TABLE II

Hearings, Staff Workers

	COVENTRY			NATIONAL			COVENTRY AS %		
	WC	*LC*	*CC*	*WC*	*LC*	*CC*	*WC*	*LC*	*CC*
7.54–6.55	6			154	20	12	3·9		
10.56–9.57	2	2		221	36	18	0·9	5·6	
11.57–10.58	4	3		293	65	22	1·4	4·6	
1959	7	8	2	254	70	41	2·8	11·4	4·9
1960	19	6	2	407	126	58	4·6	4·8	3·4
1961	23	13	2	388	120	52	5·9	10·8	3·8
1962	31	17	13	567	173	61	5·5	9·8	21·3
1963	36	25	7	663	192	83	5·4	13·0	8·4
1964	52	29	19	793	268	116	6·6	10·8	16·4
1965	84	58	23	1174	425	154	7·2	13·6	14·9
1966	54	42	37	1137	605	351	4·8	6·9	10·5
1967	88	27	14	1048	387	228	8·4	7·0	6·1
1968	78	33	9	1005	326	161	7·8	10·1	5·6
1969	96	50	29	1352	449	225	7·1	11·1	12·9

TABLE III

'Disposal Rates', Coventry and National, 1963–9

	CENTRAL AS % OF WORKS		FTA AT CENTRAL AS % OF CCS		FTA AT CENTRAL AS % OF WORKS	
Manual	Cov.	Nat.	Cov.	Nat.	Cov.	Nat.
1963	16·0	9·9	26·6	42·6	4·3	4·2
1964	12·7	10·2	52·2	46·9	6·6	4·8
1965	16·3	10·8	28·6	41·9	4·7	4·5
1966	15·3	13·5	38·9	46·1	5·9	6·2
1967	13·3	9·7	54·3	50·8	7·2	4·9
1968	12·8	12·9	36·1	39·1	4·6	5·0
1969	21·4	11·5	36·4	37·1	7·8	4·3
Staff						
1963	19·4	12·5	42·9	53·0	8·3	6·6
1964	36·5	14·6	26·3	50·0	9·6	7·3
1965	27·4	13·1	56·5	50·0	15·5	6·6
1966	68·5	30·9	64·8	73·5	44·4	22·7
1967	15·9	21·8	64·3	60·1	10·2	13·1
1968	11·5	15·7	88·9	56·1	10·3	9·1
1969	30·2	16·6	58·7	46·3	14·5	8·2

3

Going through Procedure: the Unions

Strong union organization has long existed, among both manual and white-collar employees, in the engineering industry of Coventry and district. This is particularly true of the larger factories, where the closed shop (whether or not officially recognized by management) is widespread. The Transport and General Workers' Union (TGWU) and the Amalgamated Union of Engineering and Foundry Workers (AEF) each hold somewhere over 40 per cent of the manual trade unionists in local engineering. The third largest of the local manual unions is the National Union of Vehicle Builders (NUVB), while significant membership also exists in the National Society of Metal Mechanics (NSMM), the Electrical Trades Union (ETU), and the two Sheet Metal Workers' Societies (NUSMWC and BMSMW). Other manual unions have only a small local membership in the industry, and no full-time official, but are still entitled to use procedure: the Wood-Cutting Machinists (ASWM), the Woodworkers (ASW), the Patternmakers (UPA), the Building Trade Workers (AUBTW), the Painters and Decorators (ASPD), and the General and Municipal Workers (GMWU).[1]

Among white-collar employees, union membership is shared roughly equally by four organizations: the Clerical and Administrative Workers' Union (CAWU), the Association of Clerical, Technical and Supervisory Staffs (ACTSS)—the staff section of the TGWU, previously known as the National Association of Clerical and Supervisory Staffs (NACSS), the Draughtsmen's and Allied

Technicians' Association (DATA), and the two Divisions of ASTMS.[2]

The numerical preponderance of the two main unions is reflected in utilization of procedure; and in terms of initiation of references—rather than mere participation in joint references—they virtually monopolize it. A substantial demonstration of this fact is provided by Table IV, which gives the number of references in which each union was involved in each year 1963–9. Table V presents a breakdown of union involvement in single- and multi-union references in a twelve-month period during 1969–70. These are located in the annex to this chapter.

These statistics show that each manual union participates in procedure roughly in proportion to the size of its membership. But only the two largest regularly submit references independently. In the period covered by Table V, the smaller unions appeared in total in only 7 per cent of single- or two-union references; they were all involved predominantly in the minority of references involving three or more unions. Several smaller unions appeared exclusively in such references.

Part of the explanation must be that the smaller unions commonly have a minority of members even within the individual department or workshop; in such cases it would perhaps be natural to allow the majority union to take the initiative in procedural references. The smaller unions do however have majority or even exclusive representation in certain sections or departments of some firms;[3] it is significant that the NUVB, which is probably the most often in this situation, is the only minor union involved in a sizeable number of single-union references. It is possible that the effects of size are reinforced by the strong craft background of some of the smaller societies, involving a traditional preference for reliance on workshop controls rather than procedural discussions as a means of resolving grievances. As other authors have noted, 'some strong craft unions have been reluctant to refer disputes to Procedure, regarding it as biased (one highly respected craft union leader, indeed, operated on the principle that no case should be taken up officially unless the men concerned had first struck on their own accord).'[4] This is not to suggest that officials of the two major unions do not also regard procedure as biased—for indeed they do—or that their members are necessarily reluctant to use extra-constitutional action. But a craft tradition appears to be associated with an objection in principle to involvement in procedure (which was in origin designed precisely to limit traditional craft autonomy), whereas unions of more general membership tend to view procedure more pragmatically as an often useful device.

On the white-collar side, all unions make increasing use of procedure, though there is considerable variation from year to year in the relative involvement of different organizations. If ASTMS is treated as a single unit, then from its formation it has led the white-collar field in the number of references submitted. If a distinction is made between ASTMS and DATA (largely supervisory and technical) on the one hand, and CAWU and ACTSS (largely though by no means exclusively clerical) on the other, the former customarily predominate. This may reflect a tendency of ASTMS and DATA to submit references on behalf of individual grades of staff, whereas broader-based claims are more common from ACTSS and CAWU.

In all unions, references to external procedure are submitted to the Employers' Association by the district full-time official. The exact manner in which this is handled differs however between organizations.

In the TGWU, references are processed with the minimum formality. In most cases, the senior steward at the establishment concerned merely telephones the district office to request a Works Conference. Almost automatically, the necessary arrangements are made with the Association; though where a convenor lacks experience or confidence (usually only at a smaller firm) he may receive guidance from the full-time official regarding the form a reference should take. Only in exceptional circumstances would an official consider that he has a right to refuse to pursue a question; logically, suggested one officer, some references ought to be excluded—'but you don't get results by logic in this game'.

In the AEF, the system is somewhat more formalized—largely in consequence of the requirements of the union rule-book. Applications for a Works Conference are always submitted by the factory representative to the District Secretary in writing, together with a (usually very brief) statement of the background. By rule, District Committee approval is necessary before a reference can proceed further, but locally this authority has been delegated to the District Secretary. The latter forwards the correspondence to the Divisional Organizer (whose office is in the same building), who then arranges the conference with the Employers' Association. As in the TGWU, the relevant officials almost automatically pursue any shop floor request.

In the smaller manual unions, where use of procedure is far less routine, the effective authority of the District Committee is often much greater. In the white-collar unions, by contrast, the full-time official has complete discretion; though here too, it would be wholly exceptional to refuse to pursue a membership request for a Works Conference.

The procedure for pursuing cases from Works to Local Conference varies between unions, but in most cases is broadly similar to that described above. In all unions, in the event of failure to agree at Local level, a report is made to the National Executive. It is for this body to make any reference to the final stage of procedure. The evidence would suggest that the national officials are somewhat more selective than the local, in particular having the responsibility to ensure that no claim is pressed which conflicts with national union policy.

All local unions with membership in engineering (with the minor exception of the Building Trade Workers) are affiliated to the Confederation of Shipbuilding and Engineering Unions. Its Coventry District Committee, more energetic than most, holds regular meetings; it is one of three described by Marsh as 'often . . . actively involved in local negotiations and sometimes in the making of agreements at works level'.[5] This seems to overstate the present role of Confederation locally within procedure. The District Committee does indeed act as a co-ordinating body and may even convene multi-union conferences. But it is only rarely involved in negotiations at district level (when the occasional issue of general concern arises, such as holiday dates or the application of national agreements); while at works level, the Confederation never submits references to the procedure.

The complement of officials responsible for dealing with union references varies between organizations. In the AEF, negotiations are conducted by the Divisional Organizer and his assistant (the District Secretary being responsible only for administration). The TGWU is represented in negotiations by a District Secretary and four District Organizers; while these have responsibility for a range of different industries, about four-fifths of the union's local membership is in engineering. All other unions have at most one full-time official in Coventry, responsible for both bargaining and administration.

The inflation in the conference workload has drastically reduced the amount of time that the officers of the major unions can devote to each reference. In many cases they will arrive at a conference having only the most limited knowledge of the issues involved. Experience allows them to pick up the essentials of a case in the brief discussion with shop-floor representatives before the conference commences, and to present the arguments virtually 'off the cuff'. Even at Local Conference—where the officer will already be familiar with the reference—there is no time for detailed preparation of the case, at least in the major unions. This contrasts sharply with the situation several years ago; and some officials certainly dislike the need to argue a case 'on the notes' without sufficient preparation.

The increased workload also entails that in the larger unions the official can take no continuing interest in the references he handles. Of necessity, after writing a brief report on one conference he must forget it as he turns to the next. Where a reference is adjourned to allow further domestic discussion, the union office is rarely informed if a settlement is reached. Even if a Works Conference ends in failure to agree, it is unusual for a Local to be requested immediately; normally the shop-floor representatives will report back to their members, who must then decide whether to ask the official to pursue the case further.

Finally, the rise in conference workloads has an inevitable impact on union attitudes to procedure: the official's job is tolerable only if he can render himself in normal circumstances dispensable, encouraging his members to rely on their own experience and their own resources. In at least one respect, this approach is institutionalized: AEF national policy prevents the reference of disputed payment-by-results times or prices to procedure, on the grounds that these ought under the national agreement to be mutually agreed on the shop floor. Some officials in other unions profess a similar policy, voicing the fear that if piecework claims were pursued successfully in procedure, the number of such references would quickly snowball.

This desire to foster shop-floor self-sufficiency creates ambivalence in official union attitudes. As will be argued in a later chapter, the encouragement of self-reliance among shop-floor bargainers—in the light of the *type of issue* characteristic of this bargaining process—renders the whole status of existing procedural discussions problematic.

The need to force decision-making responsibility more firmly back to the workshop is one—though not of course the only—factor underlying the recent trade union insistence on fundamental alterations in engineering procedure. Yet, paradoxically, the unprecedented level of procedural activity in recent years demonstrates that unions find procedure useful. Why this is so will be discussed in a later chapter, after the role of management has been analysed.

REFERENCES

1. As a consequence of amalgamation, a number of these unions have recently changed their titles or ceased independent existence.
2. Estimates of union coverage are based on a census conducted in 1968. While membership details relate to all engineering establishments, there is no reason to assume that proportions in federated firms would differ significantly. The only probable exceptions are the sectional craft societies, which may have a higher than average proportion of members in smaller non-federated establishments.
3. See for example the table of membership distribution in a Coventry car factory, given by H. A. Turner, G. Clack and G. Roberts, *Labour Relations in the Motor Industry*, Allen and Unwin, 1967, p. 197; and the description of the same factory by Clack, *Industrial Relations in a British Car Factory*, C.U.P., 1967, pp. 27–8.
4. Turner, Clack and Roberts, op. cit., p. 252.
5. *Industrial Relations in Engineering*, p. 30.

ANNEX

TABLE IV

Union Involvement in Procedure, 1963–9

	1963	*1964*	*1965*	*1966*	*1967*	*1968*	*1969*
MANUAL:							
AEF	55	106	164	150	148	180	203
TGWU	45	93	139	141	148	196	202
NUVB	12	12	23	23	23	18	26
NSMM	8	18	29	23	18	28	24
ETU	7	9	16	13	13	14	17
BMSMW	1	2	3	3	5	4	12
NUSMWC		2	4	8	5	1	10
UPA		1	1	3	7	4	10
AUFW		2	1	3	2 (merged into AEF)		
ASWM		2	4	2	3	1	3
ASW	1						3
ASPD					1	1	
GMWU			1			1	
STAFF:							
ACTSS	11	14	23	15	21	24	22
CAWU	8	14	29	19	28	22	40
DATA	19	15	30	15	33	22	33
ASTMS (A)	4	2	15	11	9	14	23
ASTMS (1)	N/A	N/A	N/A	17	29	28	36

TABLE V

Union Involvement in Single- and Multi-Union References

Number of Unions Involved in Reference:

	1	2	3	4	5+	Total
MANUAL:						
AEF	59	99	20	5	12	195
TGWU	67	97	19	5	12	200
NUVB	7	4	5	1	8	25
NSMM	1	2	12	2	10	27
ETU	2	1	3	4	9	19
BMSMW		1	1	1	8	11
NUSMWC			1		9	10
UPA			2	2	3	7
ASW					3	3
ASWM					3	3
(Total Refs.)	(136)	(102)	(21)	(5)	(12)	(276)
STAFF:						
ACTSS	8	7	1	1		17
CAWU	26	6	2	1		35
DATA	19	2	1	1		23
ASTMS (A)	13	1	2	1		17
(Total Refs.)	(66)	(8)	(2)	(1)		(77)

4

Going through Procedure: the Companies

Employment in Coventry in 1969 totalled 174,000; while in those trades which might be roughly categorized as engineering ('engineering and electrical goods', 'vehicles and aircraft', and 'metal goods') the number was 111,000, or 64 per cent of the total.[1] Of the latter, about 77 per cent worked in federated firms, affiliated to the Coventry and District Association.

In 1969 the Association had 89 member firms, employing a total of 97,000 workers; two-thirds of these companies, including all the largest, were situated in Coventry itself.[2] Average employment within member firms was thus over 1,000—compared with an average of somewhere over 350 in the whole Engineering Employers' Federation. The median employment in Coventry federated firms was 200; but 19 companies (21 per cent) employed over 1,000 workers each and accounted for 84 per cent of local federated employment. These figures may be compared with data for the EEF nationally: the median employment is 160; 10 per cent of federated firms have over 1,000 employees; and these account for 75 per cent of federated employment.[3] Coventry thus differs from the national pattern of EEF membership in the presence of an unusual concentration of very large productive units—which is in turn a reflection of the character of engineering production locally.[4]

Marsh and Jones, in their study of Central Conference references in 1959, have indicated the effect of company size on the chances of involvement in the final stage of procedure:

> Large engineering firms are undoubtedly the most likely to find themselves at Central Conference, and those with over 1,000 manual workers somewhat more likely than their employing power would suggest. Small or medium-sized firms are involved in Central Conference less frequently and approximately in proportion to their numbers of manual workers. Very small firms employing fewer than fifty manual workers and comprising almost one-third of the Employers' Federation membership did not appear at all at York in 1959.[5]

The minority of firms with over 1,000 employees, which (in 1959) accounted for 58 per cent of manual employment in federated firms, were involved in 64·7 per cent of cases at York. These largest firms thus showed an index of 'Central Conference-proneness' (i.e. the ratio of Central Conference involvement to size of labour force) of 112. Frequency of appearance at York was also found to vary with type of engineering production; thus motor vehicle firms were highly Central Conference-prone, with an index of 155.[6]

It is not difficult to suggest an explanation for such findings. Numerous industrial sociologists have posited a 'size effect' whereby job satisfaction declines and conflict rises with increasing size of enterprise—an effect attributable primarily to the bureaucratization necessary within the larger organization.[7] One aspect of this size effect which might reasonably be anticipated would be a greater readiness of workers in the large organization, in comparison to those in smaller firms, to raise grievances and pursue these in the external procedure. In addition, the level of authoritative decision-making in the large company is likely to be at several removes from the shop floor, and hence nearer the level of external procedure. In terms of union organization also, it has been argued that 'stewards are still a phenomenon of the larger firm . . . In small establishments the extreme informality of relationships between managements and workers makes formal shop steward organization a relative rarity.'[8] Equally, the high Central Conference-proneness of the car manufacturers might be anticipated, first because of the large size of the average establishment, and also because of the much publicized dispute-proneness of the British motor industry.[9]

The statistics of hearings on Coventry references, tabulated in an earlier chapter, show that use of procedure *at all levels* has, since 1964, been above—and often considerably above—the national average in relation to numbers employed (since the Coventry Association represents some 5 to 6 per cent of federated employment). This might perhaps be taken as an indication of the operation of the 'size effect' on the behaviour of the district as a whole; though the relatively low use of procedure in the years before 1964 would then require explanation.

A more fundamental problem is raised by the distribution of references *among* companies. Analysis of references in the years 1967–9 shows that Coventry firms with over 1,000 manual employees are marginally *less* likely to be involved at York, relative to the size of their labour force, than are smaller companies; while local motor-car firms are only marginally more likely than other companies to appear at Central Conference.[10] If Central Conference-proneness is calculated to include references for all employees (and not merely, as in the study by Marsh and Jones, manual workers), Coventry car firms appear no different from other companies; and the very largest establishments, with over 5,000 employees, are slightly under-represented at Central Conference relative to the size of their labour force.[11] It can thus be said that the findings of Marsh and Jones in a national analysis of 1959 Central Conferences are not closely reflected in recent Coventry experience.

One factor requiring emphasis is the wide range of experience subsumed under statistics of average Central Conference-proneness. Considerable variations may be discovered in the involvement within procedure of individual firms of similar size and technology; in the involvement of the same company in different years; and in 'procedure-proneness' at different stages of procedure. To illustrate such variations, Table VI shows the procedure-proneness (i.e. the proportionate involvement in Coventry district references, in relation to the proportion of local federated employment covered) at Works and Central Conference, in each year 1967–9, of three car-assembly firms each employing over 5,000 manual workers.

TABLE VI

'Procedure-Proneness' of Three Coventry Companies, 1967–9

	1967		*1968*		*1969*	
	WC	*CC*	*WC*	*CC*	*WC*	*CC*
Company A	37	152	42	95	53	268
Company B	46	115	33	23	21	29
Company C	81	39	87	132	107	144

Such variation limits the significance of any average, particularly when derived from a relatively small population; factors specific to an individual company at a particular time may well distort the general pattern.[12] Nevertheless, there are certain general points that can be made about the record of Coventry firms. One problem already mentioned as requiring explanation is the rapid increase in local involvement in procedure in the 1960s, remarkable even against the background of the rising national trend. A relevant factor which has not so far been discussed is the role of the Employers' Association, and in particular its conception of the functions of procedure. Traditionally, Association policy would seem to have been to regard procedure—and in particular the higher stages—as a mechanism to be avoided wherever possible; less a means of resolving disputes than a ceremonial demonstration of managerial resolve to make no concession to a union demand considered wholly unreasonable. Presumably this tended to reinforce the view common among managements that disputes should be kept 'within the family', and that recourse to external procedure represents an admission of failure. More recently, the Association has tended to stress the contrary view, that procedure constitutes a potentially valuable service to member firms, who should not be inhibited from making use of the professional expertise of Association staff in handling references.

The absence of any marked size effect in local use of procedure may to some extent represent a differential need among managements for outside assistance in dispute handling. While the largest firms may well possess the highest density of industrial relations grievances, they are also most likely to possess experienced and professional industrial relations management; thus proportionately more grievances may be expected to be resolved domestically. Moreover, relative sophistication in industrial relations *policy*—aimed at the prevention as well as the resolution of disputes—is more likely to exist in the larger company. Here also, the domestic union negotiators are most likely to approximate in experience and status to the full-time official.

Some evidence for this interpretation is provided by the lower-than-average disposal rate of references from the larger firms: these are more likely, relative to other companies, to be involved in Central than Works Conferences.[13] This suggests that those references which enter procedure from companies in these categories are either inherently more 'difficult', or have resulted in a more inflexible 'final' stance by company or union, than is the case among member firms as a whole. It is conceivable that at a general level such a factor may explain the low disposal rate of Coventry references by comparison with national figures.

It remains to emphasize that some of the most interesting problems relating to the use of procedure arise from the contrasts in the experience of apparently similarly situated establishments. Such contrasts can be explained only in the light of differing managerial (and domestic trade-union) policies towards industrial relations, and differing conceptions of the functions of procedure. It is these factors that are analysed in the following chapter.

REFERENCES

1. Figures supplied by the Coventry office of the Department of Employment.

2. Most recent returns show an increase in local federated firms to 109; despite the withdrawal of the Rootes Motor Co. from the EEF at the end of 1969, total federated employment in Coventry is now slightly higher than the figure given in the text.
3. Information supplied by the EEF; these figures are approximate.
4. Coventry may indeed be considered unique in the size of its engineering labour force compressed into a relatively small geographical area, and thus dominating the structure of local employment. It would be surprising if this concentration did not have some effect on industrial relations, though no attempt has been made to assess this effect in this study.
5. A. I. Marsh and R. S. Jones, 'Engineering Procedure and Central Conference at York in 1959: a Factual Analysis', *British Journal of Industrial Relations*, 1964, p. 234.
6. Ibid., pp. 234–5. The concept of procedure-proneness is used to indicate the frequency with which a company is involved in procedure, measured against the size of its labour force. A firm with 2 per cent of federated employment, and involved in 1 per cent of cases at York, would show a Central Conference-proneness index of 50; if the same firm appeared in 5 per cent of cases its index would be 250.
7. For a summary of the literature see G. K. Ingham, *Size of Organization and Worker Behaviour*, C.U.P., 1970.
8. A. I. Marsh and E. E. Coker, 'Shop Steward Organization in the Engineering Industry', *British Journal of Industrial Relations*, 1963.
9. Turner, Clack and Roberts, *Labour Relations in the Motor Industry;* see also R. Blauner, *Alienation and Freedom*, Chicago, 1964, Ch. 5. For more general discussion of the effects of technology on management structure and industrial relations, see, e.g., J. Woodward, *Management and Technology*, H.M.S.O., 1958.
10. An index of Central Conference-proneness was constructed for these years on a local basis (i.e., a firm whose involvement in Coventry references at York was in exact ratio to its proportion of local federated manual employment would register 100). The indices for the following categories of company were:
    1,000+ employees: 99; 5,000+: 114; Motor cars: 105.
11. An index calculated on the same basis but covering all employees shows: 1,000+: 101; 5,000+: 95; Motor cars: 100.
12. To give one example; footnote 10 showed an index of 114 for firms with over 5,000 employees; this is derived from annual indices of 98, 93 and 150 in each year 1967–9. The index for 1969 is unusually high because of the atypical experience of Company A in Table VI. In this year, two companies sharing 22 per cent of local federated manual employment were responsible for 49 per cent of Coventry hearings at York; in such a situation, generalisation is clearly dangerous at the level of a single district.
13. Procedure-proneness for the categories listed above, in the years 1967–9 was as follows:—

	1,000+	5,000+	Motor cars
Works	90	83	61
Central	99	114	105

5

The Functions of Procedure

The Content of Procedural Discussion: a Theoretical Framework

The study so far has concentrated on a largely straightforward account of the use of procedure in the Coventry district. It is now necessary to suggest an explanation and interpretation of the pattern of procedural usage, and to consider such broader questions as the reasons why the parties choose to utilize procedural discussions and the manner in which these contribute to the system of industrial relations in engineering: what sociologists would tend to term the 'functions' of procedure.

This is obviously a complex issue; and to tackle this in a satisfactory manner the detailed evidence of the study must be presented within a more generalized framework of reference. It is therefore necessary to begin by outlining some theoretical arguments concerning the operation of procedure.

A disputes procedure, according to one author, 'is many things: a face-saving device, a power instrument for making deals, a judicial system, or a laboratory for developing negotiating issues, leadership skills and political alliances'.[1] This is to say that a procedure is *multi-functional*: the parties involved in any reference may be using it for several different purposes; and the use of procedure may have consequences not deliberately intended by any of the parties. At the same time, procedural discussion is only one of several means by which those involved in industrial relations may pursue their objectives; for example, the aim of obtaining some specific change in conditions of employment may be pursued by means of purely domestic negotiations, by informal contacts between union official and management, or by the application of some form of sanction. Thus formal procedural discussion constitutes one of several *functional alternatives*; and the choice of this particular alternative requires explanation. Analysis of the use of procedure in any single case is therefore a considerable task, while sensible generalization is fraught with hazards. The discussion which follows is therefore necessarily tentative.

It is first necessary to consider analytically the processes involved in engineering procedure. One authority has suggested that:

> For all its apparent complexity, the ideas which underlie engineering procedure are relatively simple. It serves to carry out three functions. In the first place it is a 'safety valve' against the spread of disputes in an industry in which union/employer relationships are primarily domestic; in the second, it is a means of recognizing the negotiating rights of trade unions in the workshop while at the same time bringing strong pressure to bear against their misuse; thirdly, it is a means by which, in the event of failures to settle issues at workshop level, conciliatory forces outside the factory can be brought to bear on the situation.[2]

All three of these functions reflect a common purpose, which is implicit in the very title 'provisions for avoiding disputes': the peaceful resolution of differences arising in the workplace. Yet the agreements which specify the institutions of procedure offer no precise guidance as to the nature of the resolution process. Are workplace differences to be resolved through a process of adjudication, conciliation, or bargaining?

The judicial model is suggested by many of the accoutrements of engineering procedure; the formalized terms of reference and findings, the process of multi-stage hearings, the culmination at the several 'courts' at Central Conference. A judicial analogy is also apparent in some official accounts of the operation of procedure: the aim of 'bringing out all the underlying facts' as a basis for 'judging the merits of the trade union claim'.[3] Yet the model is fundamentally unsatisfactory: first because the proceedings are conducted by representatives—however detached from the immediate focus of the dispute—of one of the parties; second, because a positive outcome requires some formula acceptable to both parties; third, because of the fervent insistence (in theory at least) that no decision may set a precedent for any future case.[4]

These criticisms suggest the perspective of procedural discussion as a form of conciliation: an interpretation embraced by Marsh in his categorization of engineering procedure as a form of 'employer conciliation'. Yet this model too is to some extent misleading—again because the conduct of proceedings is in the hands of an 'outsider' but hardly a 'neutral'. The complex role of the Chairman has been indicated by Munns:

> Although the aim of referring the disagreement on a 'domestic' issue to the association is to seek reconciliation of opposing views, the function of the association is not that of an independent conciliator. Nor is it simply to support the member employer, right or wrong. The association representative analyses the employer's case, considers it in the light of the practice of other member firms in the district or industry, and in the framework of the policy of the association and formal agreements, and advises the member whether to concede a claim, hold firm, or compromise. He is, of course, also bound to take into account practical considerations such as the strength of the employer's will to resist the claim and his capacity to withstand a stoppage of work if agreement cannot be reached.[5]

The concept of a conciliator—both in common discourse and in the industrial relations context—typically denotes a neutral outsider; by extension the concept of 'joint conciliation' may be applied to a body equally representative of the disputing parties, detached from the immediate issue, whose partialities may be considered mutually neutralizing; but a process of unilateral conciliation is a conceptual monstrosity.

If engineering procedure is not to be treated as a social

process wholly *sui generis* one alternative remains: its conception as a form of bargaining (conceived broadly as a political process as well as an economic one). Such a model accords well with at least the unofficial viewpoint of the parties to procedure themselves.

One merit of the bargaining model is its flexibility, since the bargaining process typically involves several analytically distinct patterns of relationship. Thus Walton and McKersie have defined four separate sub-processes:

> Four systems of activity, each with its own function for the interacting parties, its own internal logics, and its own identifiable set of instrumental acts or tactics . . . The first subprocess is *distributive bargaining*, its function is to resolve pure conflicts of interest. The second, *integrative bargaining*, functions to find common or complementary interests and solve problems confronting both parties. The third subprocess is *attitudinal structuring*, and its functions are to influence the attitudes of the participants toward each other and to affect the basic bonds which relate the two parties they represent. A fourth subprocess, *intraorganizational bargaining*, has the function of achieving consensus within each of the interacting groups.[6]

The distinction presented here between 'distributive' and 'integrative' bargaining reflects in turn an analytical division within the subject-matter of bargaining between what are termed 'issues' and 'problems'. Issues are defined as questions in the settlement of which any outcome that benefits one party involves a corresponding loss for the other. All that bargaining can therefore achieve is to determine how the gains and losses are *distributed*. Problems on the other hand permit an outcome advantageous to both parties; the bargaining process *integrates* the parties by bringing them together in search of a common solution of mutual benefit. Whereas issues are typically resolved by some form of compromise—the paradigm of 'bargaining' —the resolution of problems involves a more complex process:

> The agreement involved in compromise is to be distinguished from that involved in integration. In the former case, each part is able to identify the precise extent of his losses and gains; in the

> latter, new alternatives are accepted of such a kind as to render it extremely difficult to discern the balance between concessions made and concessions received.[7]

In practice, most bargaining situations involve elements of both processes; there are few pure issues or pure problems. Nevertheless, it is normal for a situation at least to approximate to one or other 'ideal type'.

The Evidence of the Case Studies

This conceptual framework may be applied to the content of procedure, as represented by the 33 cases described in the Appendix. At the outset one may note the relative infrequency of what are sometimes termed 'disputes of right'—conflicts relating to the application of agreements. Questions of interpretation did indeed arise in five cases (21–24 and 28): but in most of these references the point at issue was not whether the company was *obliged* by the terms of an agreement to make the proposed concession, but whether the *spirit* of the agreement made this appropriate—a question of 'fairness' rather than 'justice'. Equally rare is serious argument regarding the facts of the case; only in four references (15, 19, 20 and 33) was this an important point at issue. Hence the content of procedural references would appear to underline the inadequacy of judicial models: questions of law and of fact, supposedly the sole concern of the judicial process, are rarely at issue in procedure.

Equally significant is the infrequency of obvious problems as opposed to issues. Only four references stand out as possessing important problem-solving content (11, 14, 15 and 33); and all would appear to fall within the category which Walton and McKersie term 'mixed situations'—cases involving 'significant elements of conflict *and* considerable potential for integration'.[8] By contrast, the majority of references comprise primarily win-or-lose (or compromise) issues: and in particular pay claims, the clearest basis for distributive bargaining.

It is reasonable to ask whether this composition of references in procedure reflects the general distribution of 'questions arising' on the shop floor, or whether there is selectivity in the entry of different types of questions into formal external procedure. A definitive answer would require an extensive investigation of patterns of domestic bargaining, to provide an adequate basis for comparison. But a tentative answer is suggested by an analysis of records of domestic negotiations, in the years 1967–9, at one of the largest of Coventry federated firms. These show that while only 42 per cent of recorded questions discussed domestically were wage claims, 67 per cent of Works Conferences came within this category. Thus wage claims, having reached the higher levels of domestic procedure, were three times as likely to reach Works Conference as non-wage questions: 13·3 per cent of wage claims, having reached a sufficient level in the managerial hierarchy to be formally recorded, went on to external procedure, as against only 4·8 per cent of other questions. At one firm at least, therefore, there is considerable selectivity favouring the entry of pure issues into procedure.

Any explanation of this selectivity, while necessarily conjectural, has implications for the understanding of procedure as such. First, it may be suggested that 'judicial' questions are likely to be settled outside the formal procedure. National negotiators themselves normally give attention to problems of implementation of their agreements; and where any difficulties which arise affect a number of establishments they will normally lead to guidelines agreed, formally or informally, between the Association and the Confederation at district level. Such agreement occurred (between the Association and the one union principally concerned) in the case of the Apprentices and Junior Workers' Agreement, discussed in the Appendix; hence the references pursued in procedure were not primarily regarded as 'questions of law'. Where a conflict of interpretation arises at an individual company, management would normally seek guidance from the Association (and stewards, from their district official); informal contacts would normally obviate the need for any procedural reference. Disputes involving 'questions of fact' might also be expected to be resolved informally and usually domestically. When such cases do enter procedure—as with the few which occurred during the case studies—this typically reflects abnormal problems of communication within the union and/or management.

The frequency with which distributive issues, in particular pay claims, enter engineering procedure has led some employer spokesmen to refer ironically to 'provisions for conceding wage increases'; and one commentator has suggested that 'the handling of domestic disputes has become a form of local wage negotiation'.[9] While such remarks often imply criticism of the use made by trade unions of procedure, they constitute an appropriate comment on the nature of procedural discussion itself. It seems likely that pay claims (with the exception of straightforward payment-by-results prices) are less likely than the generality of questions to be resolved domestically. One reason is the overt nature of any concession: a settlement must be formally notified (if only to the wages office), and it is in this area that lower management is most likely to be subject to controls from above and least likely to have authority to make concessions in the early stages of domestic discussion. Management may also be less ready to treat a wage claim as requiring rapid redress than it would, say, a grievance concerning working conditions. Another reason is the temptation for both sides to adopt 'unrealistic' positions at the outset of negotiations, in the hope that any eventual compromise will be closer to the desired figure. This is because it is often particularly difficult to predict with confidence the eventual point of settlement of a wage demand. Conventions as to what is 'reasonable' are sufficiently precise in the case, say, of hours of work or length of holidays to permit an accurate estimate of what management will eventually offer and the union accept; with a pay claim this is not the case, and it is far harder to assess the seriousness of the union's initial aspirations and management's response. The process of mutual accommodation is thus more likely to be complex and protracted, and to spill over into external procedure.

A factor of more general relevance is that procedure by its very nature may encourage the submission of such issues as wage claims, while offering a less appropriate context for discussion of more complex problems. To return to the theoretical arguments of Walton and McKersie:

> The techniques for fostering the integrative process are generally the reverse of the techniques for implementing the distributive process. Typically, in both processes the parties start with differences in viewpoints, perceptions, and tentatively preferred solutions. In both processes they are seeking to realize the most satisfaction possible. But the means and manner by which they settle these differences and obtain the most satisfaction possible out of the interaction are quite different. The implementing techniques for these two processes generally stand in an antithetical relationship. In brief, integrative bargaining is tentative and exploratory and involves open-communication processes, whereas distributive bargaining involves adamant, directed, and controlled information processes.[10]

Engineering procedure normally accords with the latter description. Walton and McKersie suggest that integrative bargaining is facilitated where the agenda specifies a problem in a form which does not presuppose one party's preferred solution; where adequate time exists for a careful exploration of alternative approaches; and where a series of related problems can be considered in conjunction. But it is characteristic of procedure that isolated questions should be discussed, normally under highly specific terms of reference; that conferences should handle references with expedition; and, normally, that the preferred objective of the initiating party should be clearly and firmly defined at the outset. In itself, this might be expected to inhibit the submission to procedure of problems appropriate for integrative bargaining.

Such inhibition is reinforced by the existence of alternative means of handling such problems. Marsh and

McCarthy have noted, in their discussion of the increasing conference workload, that

> The pressure which runaway use of procedure has created for the *formal* machinery would have been much greater if there had not also been a considerable increase in *informal* conferences at local level. Such meetings were at one time rare in the industry. But now it is relatively uncommon to find that, if workshop grievances prove intractable, there has been no attempt to settle them informally by the firm and the trade union official concerned. In many cases, the local employers' association is either a party to such discussions or is kept informed about them (in strict accordance with the spirit of procedure which discourages federated employers from negotiations without their own trade union representative being present) but in other cases, there has grown up a tendency for firms to establish personal contact with trade union officials whose role has often become one of conciliator between their own members and their members' employers.[11]

Munns has added that 'in the Coventry Engineering Employers' Association it is estimated that 20 per cent of meetings with trade unions are outside the procedure'.[12] More recently the proportion has increased, as Table VII indicates, some 30 per cent of conferences held under Association auspices being informal.

TABLE VII

Number of Informal Works Conferences, 1966–9

	Manual	*Staff*	*Total*
1966	129	24	153
1967	119	40	159
1968	85	48	133
1969	104	49	153

What is not immediately apparent is the qualitative difference between references discussed at formal and informal Works Conferences. Table VIII compares the subject matter of a random sample of 250 informal conferences with the subjects of formal Works Conferences in 1968 and 1969.

TABLE VIII

Subjects of Informal Conferences and Works Conferences (in Percentages)

	Informal	*Formal*
Wages	32	73
Conditions and Holidays	6	11
Discipline and Redundancy	12	5
Procedural Matters	25	11
Other	25	

One obvious feature of this distribution is that only a minority of informal references involves the basic 'economic' issues of wages and conditions; more specifically, the 2:1 ratio of wage to non-wage references in formal procedure is here reversed.

Also noteworthy is the composition of references within each of the categories listed in Table VIII. Over half the wage references discussed at informal conferences concern payment by results, but only a small minority of these relate to individual job prices (and to some extent, this minority represents the consequences of the AEF's refusal to raise individual piecework disputes in formal procedure). The majority concern general piecework problems, or proposals for alterations in a payment system (for example, 'Piecework problems in the machine shop', or 'Request for bonus scheme for storekeepers'); in other words, what is often discussed is *how to deal* with specific payment questions. Of those references which constitute claims for straightforward increases in time rates, a significant proportion concern sections of staff employees whose right to trade-union representation is not unambiguously confirmed by any national agreement. It may therefore be said that a high proportion of pay references discussed informally involve some form of procedural problem or issue.

Of those references specifically categorized in Table VIII as procedural, a half concern complaints or problems relating to industrial relations within a whole plant or department. Most of these are raised by management, and refer either to instances of alleged unconstitutional action by union members, or to the behaviour of particular domestic union representatives. Complaints are also submitted by unions, usually alleging unreasonable delays in the company's handling of grievances, or the introduction of some change in conditions of employment without adequate consultation. And some references in this category, initiated by managements or by unions, are not explicitly accusatorial: for example, 'Industrial relations problems in the fitting department'. The other half of the procedural references divide evenly between the definition of rights, responsibilities and facilities of shop stewards and convenors; and questions of union recognition, representation and the closed shop.

The category of 'other' references comprises a heterogeneous range of questions. The principal groups involve discussion of company employment prospects and short-time working; projected changes in work arrangements and production methods; issues of labour loading, manning, and labour mobility; and complaints at the behaviour of supervisory personnel. The one factor which the majority of references in this category have in common is an incursion into the imprecise but extensive area of 'managerial prerogatives'.

It is evident that the type of reference discussed in informal conferences differs markedly from the subject-matter of formal procedure; and the composition of these references itself suggests reasons why informal treatment is preferred. First, a union may wish to raise a reference on behalf of a specific group of members (normally a staff grade), without an unambiguous right under a procedure agreement to do so. Where the local Association takes a more flexible position than the EEF nationally, the informal conference provides a substitute for formal procedural arrangements. Procedural etiquette may also require that an otherwise unexceptionable reference be treated informally, where unconstitutional sanctions are being applied.[13] Second, a reference may be raised informally because the employer wishes either to enlist the aid of the trade union in rendering its members within the company more tractable, or to obtain acquiescence or co-operation in projected changes affecting union members. Employer references, while still a minority, are far more common in informal conferences than formal procedure; in part this is because any solution to the type of question raised must normally be a genuinely agreed one. Even if the reference were specific enough to pursue formally, an ultimate failure to agree would merely give the company the right to act unilaterally—a right which in most cases it already in theory possesses as part of its 'managerial prerogatives'. Unions too may prefer to raise informally questions which affect 'managerial prerogatives'; a sympathetic response is perhaps more likely in this context than in formal procedure. Third, and more generally, either party may wish to discuss what are obviously problems rather than issues, usually under terms of reference far less specific than would be acceptable within formal procedure. In this way, the informal Works Conference constitutes the normal setting, above domestic level, for integrative bargaining.[14]

The Uses of Procedure

The question posed at the outset of this chapter may now be framed more precisely: in what ways does formal procedure in engineering contribute to a process which is primarily one of distributive bargaining? This may best be answered by considering first the actual intentions of the parties involved: why employers and unions *choose* to pursue an increasing number of questions through external procedure.

An obvious preliminary point is that only a small minority of questions arising within any establishment actually reach Works Conferences; external procedure is anything but the statistically normal mechanism whereby the parties resolve such questions. It is thus necessary to consider in what ways the minority of questions which are not resolved domestically form a distinctive group. It has already been seen that 'issues' are far more likely than 'problems' to reach formal Works Conferences; even so, the great majority of issues are disposed of domestically. It is tempting to suppose that those which do enter external procedure are in some sense peculiarly difficult. However, while a problem can possess inherent difficulty which inhibits resolution, with issues it is typically the protagonists, and the pressures they are under, rather than the question itself that are 'difficult'. A genuine problem may offer no obvious solution, however conciliatory the parties to the discussions; but with a distributive issue, the possible range of any settlement is defined at the outset by the initial positions of the parties. Difficulty in reaching agreement is a direct consequence of the bargaining stances of the two sides. Thus where an issue enters external procedure it would seem to be the behaviour of the bargainers, reflecting the particular pressures upon them at the time, rather than the subject-matter of their bargaining, which is primarily responsible.

Since the bargaining relationship necessarily involves a process of mutual interaction, any analysis which treats each party in isolation involves inevitable distortion. Nevertheless, the purposes of each party provide a natural starting point for analysis: what induces each side in certain domestic negotiations to reject the final offer of the other; and, having failed to agree, to choose procedure as opposed to extra-constitutional mechanisms as a means of seeking a more acceptable outcome? As almost all references to formal Works Conference are initiated by trade unions, it is reasonable to consider the union position first.

An obvious factor underlying the use of procedure by trade unions is the formal obligation under the national agreement to exhaust procedure before resorting to any form of sanctions. Unions officially accept that 'procedure agreements embody promises and therefore should not be broken by any union representative'.[15] Despite some ambivalence in practice, this certainly serves to inhibit unions from giving official support or encouragement to the use of unconstitutional sanctions by their members, and leads them to treat procedural discussions as the 'normal' means of processing grievances. Yet this does not explain why engineering unions—despite regular and often bitter criticism of the procedure agreement—have remained signatories to it; why indeed they accept the need for some type of formal procedure and have refrained (at least until the most recent discussions) from any serious threats of renunciation as a bargaining tactic in achieving alterations in the 1922–55 agreement.[16]

Union commitment to the use of procedure has to be related to its value as a means of achieving results. Marsh has argued that:

> despite continued trade union objection of principle they have greatly profited from the operation of the system and the cutting edge of their opposition has been blunted by the fact that engineering employers, without conceding any major part of the position they originally took up in 1898, have, in practice, been willing to allow the system to evolve informally along more liberal lines than unions might once have anticipated.

He goes on to suggest that there has been a

> tendency of employers to allow increasingly free use of Procedure to handle any issues which trade unions have wished to raise, and [a] development among managements, local associations and in the Federation of conciliatory attitudes towards workshop claims. Engineering has, partly by formal, but mainly by informal means, moved with the times. It is difficult to argue today that, in practice, the engineering system is not, in the eyes of the parties involved in it, a generally stable and acceptable one.[17]

Marsh's main thesis is that employers have been flexible in exercising their formal rights in respect of 'managerial functions'; yet, as has been seen, questions which fall within this category are rarely the subject of formal procedural discussion in Coventry. But in the more straightforward issues which predominate at Works and Local Conferences, employers do indeed show evidence of flexibility. An attempt has been made, in Table IX, to evaluate the outcome of the 33 cases studied, indicating the extent to which the union appeared to succeed, in external procedure, in inducing the company to move from its own final domestic position towards that of the union. Not too much faith should be placed in these figures: such evaluation is wholly subjective and is a highly hazardous enterprise. The 'final' domestic position of either party may represent an interim bargaining stance rather than a serious aspiration; an apparent union 'success' in procedure may merely represent the formal acceptance of an offer made 'off the record' in domestic discussion; the eventual settlement may be intrinsically difficult to evaluate. But such an analysis, however dubious its reliability, is better than none at all.

TABLE IX

Outcome of References to Procedure: Union 'Success'

		Large Extent	*Significant Extent*	*Little*	*Not at All*	*Total*
MANUAL:	Pay	6	6	2	2	16
	Other	1	1		2	4
YOUTHS:	Pay		1	1	2	4
STAFF:	Pay	2	4			6
	Other		1	1	1	3
TOTAL		9	13	4	7	33

These figures suggest that while procedural discussion yields only limited results in respect of non-wage references, most wage issues result in significant gains for the union. As one full-time officer (himself highly critical of many features of the present procedure) admitted, most of his members seemed to have considerable faith in the system, precisely because a high proportion of references do result in acceptable settlements. It is unclear how typical this situation is of the national pattern; it would not perhaps be surprising if Coventry workers were more acquiescent in the existing procedure than workers in some other areas, for local engineering technology and payment structures lead to more pay claims and fewer 'craft' issues in procedure than the national average. This presumably means that the problems of reaching an acceptable compromise are less often aggravated by major conflicts of principle.

It should be added that, even where procedural discussions fail to bring any significant concession from the company, this does not necessarily mean that they are of no use to the union. Table IX indicates that in about a third of the cases studied the company conceded little or nothing in procedure: the union either accepted what had been offered domestically, with minimal improvements, or else allowed the issue to 'die a natural death' after failure to agree. In most of these cases, the evidence suggests that the full-time official considered his members' position in some respect a weak one, but nevertheless pursued the claim through procedure as a token gesture, a substitute for more vigorous action. 'Going through the motions' can serve to reduce the intensity with which a grievance is experienced—acting as a safety-valve, a means of 'letting off steam' and thus removing potentially explosive pressures. Or as one author has put it, a little less cynically: 'procedures both give the workers an opportunity to express themselves and also require the directors of their work lives to hear and to consider their problems seriously.'[18]

The use of procedure in such circumstances may also be viewed as a reflection of the process which was referred to, in the previous theoretical discussion, as 'intra-organizational bargaining'. Such bargaining is seen by Walton and McKersie as an inevitable consequence of what they term the negotiator's 'boundary role'.[19] By this they mean that there is typically a gap between what the union members want and expect, and what the company is willing to offer, and it is the officer's task to bring these two dimensions into congruence. The most manifest aspect of this task is to induce management to revise its offer; but in most cases this will still fall short—often considerably so—of the workers' aspirations. The second aspect of the officer's task is therefore to induce the members to revise their own expectations and accept the offer. Since the full-time official in engineering normally becomes involved only after failure to agree domestically, it would be surprising if there were not Works Conferences at which he considers his members' demands unattainable and is more concerned to change *their* attitudes than those of management.

The union officer may conduct such intra-organizational bargaining in either an active or a passive manner. An active strategy requires the official to inform his members at the outset that their demands are 'unrealistic' and to persuade them to lower their aspirations; the passive strategy is formally to pursue the 'unrealistic' demand, allowing 'the pressure to change the aspiration to emanate from the environment and the bargaining process itself rather than from the negotiator'.[20]

The latter strategy would seem to possess the greater attractions for most union officials. As has been seen, they do not normally consider it their function to refuse to press 'hopeless' cases on behalf of their members. Three main reasons may be suggested: the role of the union officer is overtly defined in terms of service to his members; he cannot necessarily predict with certainty that any specific demand will prove hopeless;[21] and normally he has no wish unnecessarily to create aggrieved sections of membership. Procedure relieves the official of the need to persuade the members directly to moderate their claims; the employer representatives, by mounting a solemn display of determined resistance, perform this task for him. Thus procedure can be used, in the words of one union negotiator, to 'put on a show for the members': the officer goes through all the motions of pressing the claim forcefully; if the company offers a concession, so much the better, but if it remains unyielding the domestic representatives may well accept that their demands are unattainable. In such a case, in addition, the delay inherent in procedure may well de-fuse an initially explosive situation; the official thus avoids union involvement in a dispute which, he considers, cannot be won.

Yet, as has been seen, procedure does in most cases

provide unions with more concrete results. In itself this would appear a sufficient explanation of union readiness to fail to agree domestically and to take references into external procedure. The question then arises why companies often make concessions in external procedure which they fail to make domestically. A related question is why concessions are made at the higher levels of procedure which are not forthcoming at Works Conference.

Two explanations are frequently voiced by the parties involved. Employers are likely to suggest that this process demonstrates precisely those functions which procedure is designed to perform. Managements are able to consider the union case in an atmosphere removed from workshop emotions; in a complex case, they may hear the union arguments set out for the first time in comprehensive form; and they are exposed to the persuasive influence of Association officials and (at the highest levels of procedure) fellow employers. Undoubtedly these factors are at times important in inducing a company to revise its domestic position. But the writer's view—admittedly impressionistic—on the basis of the conferences attended, is that these are not the typical reasons for management concessions in procedure.

Trade unionists for their part often attribute such management behaviour to deliberate delaying tactics: arguing that while negotiations over a wage claim continue, a company is relieved of the need to pay any increase, and that prolonged discussions are therefore in the employer's financial interests. While deliberate delay may occur at times, this is not however necessarily of benefit to a company, since pay increases are often backdated in such circumstances. There was no clear evidence in any of the cases studied of deliberate delaying tactics by management (though it is not altogether clear what would count as evidence); at the same time, in some of these cases it appeared that the need for reference to external procedure was the result primarily of real though unintentional delay and indecision in the formulation of a company response to union demands.[22]

However, two further factors are probably of greater importance in explaining concessions made by companies in external procedure. Often the delay involved is inherent in the process of managerial decision-making itself. In many larger companies, the manager with authority to make a particular concession may become involved in negotiations only when a reference reaches Works (or even Local) Conference. The delegation of responsibility requires that domestic discussions should be conducted by a subordinate who, pressed to concede a claim with important policy implications, is obliged to fail to agree.[23] Delay until external procedure before formulating the company position may also reflect problems of intra-organizational bargaining analogous to those discussed with reference to the union official. Certain concessions may require the prior authorization of the managing director or even the board; or it may be politic to win the consent of particular line managers or staff functionaries. Such approval may often be forthcoming only after the union has demonstrated its determination by pressing the claim forcefully within procedure. Procedure can also provide a personnel manager with a justification, or at least an excuse, for a concession which he hesitates to propose on his own initiative: if it can be presented as the result of advice or pressure from the Employers' Association, he is to some extent protected against criticism from other members of management.[24]

In addition, the dynamics of the bargaining process itself may inhibit settlement before Works, Local or even Central Conference. The essence of distributive bargaining is that each party commits itself more or less firmly to a position; then, in the light of the strength of its own commitment and its assessment of it's opponent's, modifies this position until a compromise is reached. Refusal to move towards compromise in domestic discussions is one means whereby each party can attempt to convince the other of its own determination and hence, hopefully, induce the maximum concessions from its opponent. A manager, for example, may consider a union demand extravagant and refuse to commence the process of give-and-take until it is moderated; or he may be uncertain of the strength of feeling underlying the claim, and stand firm initially in order to test the union's commitment. He may also fear that whatever offer is made domestically (or in the early stages of external procedure) will be rejected, and may therefore hold some concessions in reserve for later negotiations. Such an assumption may in many circumstances be justified; but, as suggested below, in other cases it may act as a self-fulfilling prophecy.

Similar factors may induce a union to adopt an uncompromising stance at particular stages of procedure. Of course, any settlement requires that at some stage one—or more usually, both—parties must modify their initial commitments. An essential characteristic of collective bargaining is that it is never possible to predict with certainty who will be the first to move towards compromise, in what manner, and at what point of time (though, as is suggested below, past experience will have considerable influence on both parties). One important problem is that once either party has committed itself firmly to a particular position, any significant concession may involve loss of face. The existence of a multi-stage procedure, with delay between each stage, makes it easier for each side to modify an earlier commitment without undue embarrassment. In itself, this factor may induce either side to delay until a later conference an agreement which might in principle be negotiated earlier.

Procedure and the Bargaining Process

There are of course more positive ways in which procedural discussion contributes to the effectiveness of the bargaining process, but before considering these a preliminary reservation should be made. In recent years, highly sophisticated models of industrial negotiations have been constructed, often elaborating insights derived from social psychology and games theory. Such bargaining models and associated theories have been used predominantly to illuminate and analyse contract negotiations in the United States: negotiations which are of course a central feature of American industrial relations, requiring protracted series of bargaining sessions and resulting in comprehensive and legally binding contracts valid often for several years. By contrast, the engineering disputes procedure is concerned primarily with small-scale shop floor issues raised on an *ad hoc* basis, and little time is allowed for the conduct of each case. Because of the nature of the issues, elaborate subtlety of tactics is simply not worth while—and is in any case impossible because of pressure of time. If genuine bargaining is to occur it must be speedy; without rapid signs of readiness to compromise, a conference is likely to result in a summary failure to agree. This means, for example, that most of the subtle ramifications of 'commitment tactics' (analysed in detail by such writers as Walton and McKersie) must be dispensed with, or at best telescoped into an hour's exchange.

The key function of procedure as a means of dispute resolution appears to lie in its creation of an artificial social situation. This artificiality is immediately apparent to the observer of a formal conference, and is emphasized by the contrast between the behaviour of the negotiators before its commencement and during adjournments, and their behaviour while the conference is in progress. In the former situation the opposing representatives employ first-name terms and engage in small talk or light-hearted banter; when procedural discussions commence the atmosphere alters perceptibly, and the exchanges become highly formalized. It is significant that in *both* situations the actors appear to be deliberately performing roles; if the formal courtesies of the conference itself seem artificial, the preceding bonhomie often appears equally contrived.

The contrasting behaviour before and during each conference does however seem to represent a ritual demonstration that the negotiators themselves recognize the socially contrived nature of their actions: the pre-conference banter may be seen as a form of what one sociologist has termed 'role distancing'.[25] This ritualism provides an indication that an aggressive performance by either spokesman is made solely in his role as representative of company or union: it is 'not intended personally'. In this way, it is possible to differentiate 'interpersonal' and 'inter-party' relations.[26] Such differentiation has an essential function in an effective bargaining process: the hostility which a negotiator may be obliged at times to express on behalf of his organization cannot be allowed to form the basis of overt personal enmity towards an opposing representative. Such enmity would normally make intolerable the personal position of an official who must regularly interact with his opposite number. Moreover, personal antagonism would tend to preclude any 'constructive' bargaining; this normally requires at the very least that the negotiator behave *as if*, outside the conference itself, he retains no hostility towards his adversary. And indeed, a relationship of *genuine* trust and cordiality will almost certainly make life much easier for both. One union representative who seemed unable to maintain the sophisticated differentiation between role and personal relationships was, significantly, not highly regarded as a negotiator.

As well as providing an institutionalized context for inter-organizational conflict, the artificial social situation of the formal conference can serve other functions. Just as the negotiator can dissociate himself personally from any aggressive position which he may express, so he can avoid staking his personal reputation on any demand he may make or answer he may give. In consequence, it is relatively easy to modify a commitment without loss of face: compromise is thus facilitated.

In part, procedural discussion can help resolve disputes precisely because the negotiations are conducted by outside professionals. Establishments clearly do differ in the skill and experience of domestic negotiators, and there are issues which can arise in any factory in which the involvement of an outsider can facilitate settlement—perhaps along lines not considered by those directly concerned. Often the contribution of the external representative (on either side) lies in his ability to take responsibility for a concession and thus save the face of the domestic bargainer. To this extent, procedure may achieve results precisely because it is the one formal mechanism for introducing outside officials into negotiations in an industry which exhibits an ideological commitment to domestic autonomy.[27]

There is a further relevant aspect of procedural discussion as a confrontation between spokesmen on both sides who are outside professionals: their familiarity with the actual bargaining situation and with each other as adversaries. It has been argued that 'once inside the conference room, [negotiators] all appear to become more like each other than like themselves on the outside'.[28] While an exaggeration, this does indicate the extent to which constant interaction can generate a network of common understandings and expectations. An essential feature of the bargaining process is that concessions must often be hinted at rather than explicitly proposed, so as to allow withdrawal if the opponent does not reciprocate. Mutual familiarity ensures that the subtle process of probes and cues can be compressed into a few brief exchanges; that what is not said can be as eloquent as what is; and that either side can tacitly convey a complex position in a few sentences—'in a form of shorthand', as one official put it. Moreover, the process which Walton and McKersie term 'attitudinal structuring' can become highly developed: negotiators acquire a detailed though tacit understanding of which tactics and styles of bargaining are legitimate and which are not. For negotiators who may face each other several times a week, it is obviously pointless to breach these mutual expectations for the sake of advantage in a single case. The mutual confidence engendered by this framework of shared understandings can on occasion be crucial to the resolution of a dispute.[29]

The specificity of terms of reference in procedure—which was cited earlier as a means of inhibiting 'integrative bargaining'—may, however, facilitate the settlement of distributive issues. By their often narrow definition of the question at issue, the terms of reference effectively set the parameters for eventual agreement; the area of conflict is rigidly confined. It is plausible to assume that this structure may at times moderate conflict by transforming questions of quality into questions of quantity. It is interesting, for example, that officials of both main unions suggested that irreconcilable issues of principle simply do not arise in Coventry—so long as the price is right. If procedure does indeed tend to convert 'problems' into 'issues', this may often facilitate compromise.[30] Moreover, this may suggest why many references are settled informally after an adjournment or failure to agree; procedural discussions may reveal dimensions of a problem which are not encompassed by the terms of reference and cannot appropriately be resolved in the formal setting.

Inter-Company Differences

The factors discussed so far are of *general* relevance explaining why companies and trade unions make use of external procedure. Yet, as was seen in the previous chapter, the use of procedure varies considerably between establishments. Such variations would seem to reflect sharp differences in policy and attitudes towards the use of procedure.

In some companies, a deliberate effort is made to prevent, or at least to minimize, the reference of issues to Works (or at least to Local) Conference. In consequence, the domestic procedure may be so designed that all disputes are considered by the authoritative manager before outside officials are brought in. In other firms, by contrast, he may never become involved in negotiations before Works Conference. While some managers and shop stewards are extremely jealous of their domestic autonomy, or else reluctant to 'wash dirty linen in public', and so make strenuous efforts to resolve all issues internally, others are far readier in difficult circumstances to 'pass the buck' to outsiders. Or patterns of dispute handling within a factory may develop in a less conscious and deliberate manner. If management assumes that any offer which it makes domestically is likely to be rejected in the hope of further concessions at higher levels of procedure, or if union representatives judge that any domestic proposal is probably only an initial bargaining offer, then the level of settlement is bound to escalate. In effect, these will become self-fulfilling prophecies, the expectations of each side ultimately shaping the behaviour of the other. Such a situation—in which domestic negotiation is rendered increasingly ritualistic—may eventually provoke a deliberate attempt to restructure industrial relations. Yet this means transforming expectations based on the accumulated experience of workers, managers and union representatives at all levels: a slow and difficult task.

In brief, the interaction of such factors as company industrial relations policy, the structure of authority within management and union hierarchies, the personalities of domestic negotiators, and the customary bargaining relationships—in addition to such obvious factors as production technology and company size—all help shape the degree to which any firm is involved in external procedure.

Unconstitutional Action

It was suggested above that the nature of engineering procedure may be such as to facilitate compromise by narrowing the focus of argument. Yet this same factor can give rise to a more general problem: how both sides (but particularly management) should treat references which enter external procedure. Refusal to modify the domestic position invites the charge of inflexibility, of destroying the whole point of procedure; concessions invite further references to procedure and the inhibition of domestic settlement. Precisely because most references are straightforward bargaining issues rather than questions of obvious principle, it has little meaning to say that each case should be judged on its merits. The negotiators must therefore devote much of their attention, implicitly at least, to considering the balance of forces in the case in question and the implication of the various possible outcomes for future issues.

This point has relevance for any interpretation of the significance of unconstitutional strikes and related forms of sanctions, for it casts doubt upon conventional diagnoses of such action as a breakdown in collective bargaining.

Such a perspective seems to underlie the argument of the EEF, that

> relations between the Federation and its associations and the majority of trade union officials (both local and executive) are very good. Trade union officials, in general, desire to keep to agreements, they deprecate the strike in breach of agreement and will endeavour to get the men back to work. This, however, is sometimes a lengthy process. In the first place, the local association will seek to get in touch with the local or district union official and bring every pressure on him to try and get the strikers back to work. The difficulty of making contact due to non-availability sometimes causes delay. If this approach fails, the Federation will request the appropriate member of the executive committee of the trade union to bring pressure to bear to get the men back to work. This also causes delay because members of a union executive approached in this way often consider it necessary to make their own enquiries of local officials about the facts, and often desire to consult their full executive committee before taking action. Again, it is very difficult sometimes to track down the appropriate member of the committee owing to the amount of work he himself has to do.[31]

While communications within trade unions are unquestionably open to improvement, it is doubtful whether inadequacies in this respect are the principle reasons for their failure to prevent unconstitutional action. One may note, for example, the finding of the Government Social Survey that union officers in general do not necessarily deprecate the strike in breach of agreement. In some circumstances at least, a majority considers unconstitutional action justifiable; more generally, their views parallel those of their shop stewards.[32] Thus the union organizer may sympathize with members who resort to unconstitutional action; even where he does not, he may be reluctant to confront a group of members who appear resolutely committed to action in breach of procedure. Yet formally he is indeed required to disown the breach and obtain a return to normal working. Not surprisingly, an attractive means of resolving this dilemma is simply to be 'not available' when agitated employers or Association officials seek to contact the union officer.

The TUC has recorded a different view, alleging that unconstitutional action is at times deliberately encouraged by managerial tactics: 'there are cases where employers decline to bargain adequately with the union but give way to unofficial action later: in this way they gain time, save money and discredit the union.'[33] It is difficult to deny that unconstitutional action is often taken precisely because management behaviour ensures that this is the most productive method of pursuing a claim. It seems unlikely, however, that this is often the consequence of deliberate company policy; more commonly it reflects the absence of any coherent policy. And also, more often than is generally recognized, such behaviour by management may represent the outcome of the vagaries of intra-organizational bargaining.[34]

Officially, the collective attitude of employers to unconstitutional action is unambiguous:

> The principle on which the Federation acts is that it does not, if possible, discuss a grievance, real or supposed, of men who are on strike or taking other action in breach of agreement, until they resume work. When they do this, the grievance is discussed by the normal methods of discussion and negotiation.[35]

Actual practice is somewhat more flexible. The local Association sees its primary role as providing a service to member firms; if one of these wishes to negotiate despite unconstitutional action, there will be no insistence on rigid adherence to the EEF 'line'. Certainly the criticism is heard from representatives on all sides that some employers act in the manner described by the TUC, the personnel manager who has resisted a union claim in the conference room capitulating or being overruled in the event of a strike. Not surprisingly, union officers are prone to argue that where members are offered an incentive to prefer unconstitutional action to procedural discussion, they cannot be expected to enforce a different preference.

However, there would appear to be a more fundamental reason for the regular resort to unconstitutional action, and for the ambivalent attitudes which exist on both sides. Reference was made in an earlier chapter to the general desire of union officers to foster shop-floor self-sufficiency. In part at least this may reflect a recognition that the typical reference to be pursued at Works Conference is an issue rather than a problem, and that the fundamental determinants of any settlement are the balance of power and the strength of feelings within the factory itself. Of course scope may exist for outside negotiators to discover 'integrative' solutions not perceived by the immediate protagonists; and the formal atmosphere of procedure, removed from the sometimes emotional attitudes of the shop floor, may itself facilitate the resolution of a particular deadlock. But in the generality of cases, the 'bargaining range' has already been well defined before the reference enters external procedure: domestic discussion has shaped the outline of the eventual settlement. Within these limits, if the union official contributes personally to a settlement this typically reflects either his own skill in persuading management to improve its domestic offer (or his own members that no such improvement is to be expected), or else the influence of mere entry into external procedure on mutual readiness to compromise.

In such a context, each success in achieving concessions not forthcoming in domestic negotiations is an incitement to members to make increasing use of procedure: to treat it as a sausage-machine, as one official expressed it. This is to encourage precisely the escalation in references which characterized the last decade, and to reduce the attention which the organizer can give to any specific case.

The natural response is for the union officer to attempt to minimize his own role: to insist that in general the domestic bargainers should rely on their own abilities and, if necessary, live with their own mistakes. Yet such mistakes may well give rise to overt conflict. And more generally, if the typical shop-floor difference involves a distributive issue, and more specifically a wage demand, then the ability and readiness of either side to impose sanctions, and the importance of the consequences of such sanctions, must be intimately related to the behaviour of the domestic negotiators.

If domestic self-sufficiency is encouraged, and if the possibility of sanctions exerts a powerful latent influence on negotiators, it must on any realistic view be difficult to regard as sacrosanct the peace obligation which procedure incorporates. Considered against this background, the use of sanctions, and the threat of their use, must appear as essentially a bargaining tactic: not a rupture of negotiations, but their pursuance by additional means. Dubin's argument is relevant here: 'It is common in the press to characterize a strike as a breakdown in collective bargaining. However, on closer analysis it will be found to be a continuation of collective bargaining.' It is, he suggests, 'totally unrealistic' to assume 'that collective bargaining involves only discussions of issues in a peaceful manner across a bargaining table'.[36] It seems likely that this view is—perhaps implicitly—widely shared by the practitioners of industrial relations. Where thorough domestic discussions result in failure to agree, and reference to Works Conference or unconstitutional action represent alternative options for the shop-floor union representatives, the district official might not be expected to apply great energy in defending the sanctity of procedure—particularly if sanctions do indeed produce results.

Historical comparison serves to emphasize this point. When engineering procedure was first devised, 'questions arising' within the establishment were few and far between, normally involving problems of a weighty nature. With the development of domestic bargaining in recent years as the *primary* means of determining wages and conditions, it is far less obvious that any external procedure could be expected to cope with the totality of issues unresolved at workshop level. Only if *serious* bargaining occurs domestically is it possible for the volume of external references to be controlled; yet frequently, the prospects of serious bargaining would be much reduced were the possibility of sanctions wholly absent from the background. Thus a certain tension seems inherent between the prescriptions of procedure and the realities of collective bargaining in engineering.

To summarize the point which has been argued here: the use of sanctions may be intimately related to collective bargaining as such. The nature of contemporary industrial relations in engineering ensures that most references to procedure are merely sectional pay claims which happen not to have been resolved domestically. Whatever the perspicacity and bargaining skill of external negotiators, the eventual settlement is normally shaped largely by the relative strength of the domestic protagonists and the assessment each makes of the other's determination. Sanctions applied by the party seeking substantive change may provide a show of strength or an indication of determination and thus function as an integral part of the bargaining process. 'In other words, the use of procedure and strikes in breach of procedure may be complementary rather than contradictory activities.'[37]

The general problem is accentuated in two particular circumstances. First of all, union representatives face a dilemma in the case of domestic failure to agree if the issue is considered important yet managerial concessions in external procedure are not anticipated. It has been suggested that unions normally refer issues to the higher stages of procedure in

> the hope that higher levels of employers may succeed in making their member see the problem differently, or make him amenable

> to settlement. *Unless this is likely there is little point in using procedure at all, except as a device for ventilating issues and taking off pressure felt by the union from the workplace*. . . . In the first place, if an issue has been exhaustively but reasonably bargained about without success within the factory the hope of obtaining concessions higher up the procedure diminish and attitudes are more likely to harden. Second, employers outside the factory are likely to concern themselves whether the union is asking for something that has been generally conceded by other firms. If the answer is that this is not the case, then unions naturally feel that is is better that discussion should remain at domestic level. Thirdly, there is no need for any settlement to emerge from the employer conciliation process at all.[38]

As one local officer argued, it is difficult to insist that members observe procedure simply in order to satisfy formalities, if it is apparent that nothing will be achieved except further delay. This problem is particularly acute in the case of what have been termed 'perishable' issues:[39] by refraining from action pending procedural discussions a union may allow its case to go by default.

The second and closely related category of issues comprises acts of management resisted by union members but permitted under the 'managerial functions' clause of the procedure agreement.[40] In theory, trade unions are obliged to acquiesce in a wide range of managerial decisions while pursuing any objections through procedure. In practice, companies are normally cautious in insisting on their formal rights. The extent to which an implicit *status quo* provision has been allowed to operate can alone explain why trade unions in engineering have continued to tolerate—under very different economic conditions—provisions enforced in a lock-out when over 25 per cent of workers in the industry were unemployed. Yet managerial flexibility is surely to be explained, in part at least, by an awareness that managerial prerogatives cannot be enforced insensitively without provoking unconstitutional sanctions (whether in the form of passive non-co-operation or more overt action). And where a company does insist on enforcing its 'rights'—particularly in the case of such perishable issues as dismissals—any unconstitutional action is likely to be attributed by union representatives to management's breach of the 'custom and practice' which surrounds the actual functioning of procedure.[41]

It is therefore no surprise that the references covered by the present study displayed considerable official ambivalence—on both sides—towards unconstitutional action. It would appear that in eight of the thirty-three cases, sanctions occurred in breach of procedure; but only on three occasions did company representatives refer to this in procedural discussions. The formal trade-union response in such circumstances is usually either to disown the unconstitutional action or to make some brief expression of regret while pointing to mitigating factors (though in one case studied the union official was far less apologetic, merely 'noting' the Chairman's complaint and placing the blame for the unconstitutional action on the company). Outside conference proceedings, in only one of the cases studied does the union official appear to have taken active steps to persuade his members to end their sanctions; perhaps significantly, it was obvious here that the possibilities of productive domestic negotiations had not been fully explored. But where thorough domestic discussions have already been pursued without agreement, the evidence of the study suggests that the official union response to unconstitutional action will typically range between tacit encouragement and studied detachment.

But as with the use of external procedure, so in the case of unconstitutional sanctions there are important differences between companies; and a similar complex of factors is responsible. The study revealed firms, even with similar size and technological characteristics, whose experience presented marked contrasts. In one, for example, management adhered more rigidly than most to the Federation policy of 'refusal to negotiate' while action occurred in breach of proceedure; in another, management accepted as a virtual fact of life that the unions would not refer an issue to external procedure if they considered it a matter of urgency and importance and believed that sanctions would achieve results. It is interesting that at both establishments the expectations of all parties were sufficiently stable and compatible for domestic dispute-handling to function relatively smoothly—though in the former, domestic negotiation meshed closely with the industry-wide disputes procedure, while in the latter it was largely autonomous. Both companies contrast sharply with the not uncommon situation in which the parties' expectations are incompatible, or their behaviour unpredictable, and industrial relations are accordingly far less tractable.

Concluding Remarks

The ambivalence which all parties display towards unconstitutional action reflects a dilemma inherent in any disputes procedure. To be effective, procedure must operate on the assumption that either party to any reference may modify the stance taken in domestic discussions; yet if this assumption were general, domestic settlement would be, at the very least, discouraged. Thus the view is often expressed—from all sides—that management (since it is normally the trade union which initiates a reference) should make a reasonable domestic offer and stick to it. Yet any company which adhered resolutely to this advice would certainly be accused of inflexibility. The problem is evidently to define an appropriate *degree* of flexibility and firmness; but it seems fatuous to prescribe a specific proportion of references, and impossible to specify a particular type, for which managerial flexibility is in order. There is little evidence that issues in procedure share any characteristic beyond an absence of settlement domestically; in so far as procedure is rarely a judicial process, what is in question is not a review of 'the merits of the case'. Rather, each side must assess its implications against an intricate network of economic and power relationships (in which the use of procedure and the possibility of sanctions are themselves factors), and must also consider the effect of a particular settlement on future claims.

This leads to the final point in this discussion of the functions of procedure: that the topic must be viewed firmly in context. At times, an outside observer of conference discussions must feel that he is witnessing the enactment of a ritual while the real decisions are being taken elsewhere. Procedure creates the formal meeting ground for the representatives of two contending parties, and each possesses only limited autonomy. At times, this autonomy may be so circumscribed that the strategy of each side is predetermined, and failure to agree the only possible outcome. Or the brief of either party may extend only to probing the response of the other to a possible solution which requires authorization by others outside the conference room. Only in certain cases does either spokesman have authority to concede in full the other's position. Procedure must thus be conceived as one point of intersection in an ongoing intra-and inter-organizational relationship; only in this way can its values and shortcomings be adequately comprehended.

REFERENCES

1. B. D. Mabry, *Cases in Labor Relations and Collective Bargaining*, Ronald Press, 1966, p. 89.
2. Marsh, *Industrial Relations in Engineering*, p. 112.
3. Cf. Engineering Employers' Federation, *Written Evidence*, para. 173 and Marsh and McCarthy, *Disputes Procedures in Britain*, p 11.
4. In practice, both sides are often well aware that the outcome of one sectional reference will influence the formulation and eventual settlement of analogous claims for other groups of workers. This is doubtless one reason for the inconclusive formal outcome of many references: it is felt that a settlement reached domestically after reference back may be less overt a precedent than the same settlement formally recorded at a conference.
5. V. G. Munns, *Functions and Organisation of Employers' Associations in Selected Industries*, Royal Commission Research Paper 7, Part 1, H.M.S.O., 1968, p. 46.
6. R. E. Walton and R. B. McKersie, *A Behavioral Theory of Labor Negotiations*, McGraw Hill, 1965, p. 4; emphasis in original.

7. H. D. Lasswell, 'Compromise', quoted in Walton and McKersie, op. cit., p. 128.
8. Ibid., pp. 161–2; emphasis in original.
9. Munns, *Employers' Associations*, p. 9.
10. Op. cit., pp. 144, 166.
11. *Disputes Procedures in Britain*, p. 28; emphasis in original.
12. *Employers' Associations*, p. 47. To some extent, the formality of a Works Conference is a question of degree; in some cases it may not be clear how a particular conference should be classified. In addition to informal Works Conferences, meetings may take place between management and union officials which are unrecorded—possibly without the knowledge of the Association. It would seem that the frequency of such meetings has increased, though it is of course impossible to offer statistical evidence.
13. Officially at least (but see also below), Employers' Association policy prevents formal procedural discussion in such cases. Union officials may well support this policy as a protection for their own authority.
14. Reference was made earlier (p. 42) to the records of domestic negotiations at a major federated factory in Coventry. Thirty-one per cent of informal Works Conferences at this company in the period analysed involved wage references—a proportion virtually identical to that for the whole district; this might be considered evidence that the company's experience is reasonably representative in this respect. Of recorded references discussed domestically 13 per cent of non-wage and only 8 per cent of wage questions proceeded to informal Works Conference—a selectivity the reverse of that discovered in the case of formal Works Conferences.
15. Trades Union Congress, *Report*, 1960, p. 127.
16. A noteworthy historical analogy is provided by the Amalgamated Society of Engineers in 1914; having withdrawn from the Terms of Agreement with the EEF it found itself obliged to renew its commitment to the provisions for avoiding disputes which the agreement had incorporated.
17. *Industrial Relations in Engineering*, p. 214.
18. J. W. Kuhn, *Bargaining in Grievance Settlement*, Columbia University Press, 1961, p. 23. Such a use of procedure will of course only succeed if the workers concerned *believe* that their demands are being pursued seriously; emotions are likely to be heightened if it is felt that the negotiators are simply going through the motions. But it might be added that workers themselves, having raised a demand which they are not prepared to press to the point of a strike, may see reference to procedure as a face-saving way of burying the issue.
19. Op. cit., p. 284.
20. Ibid., p. 306.
21. Officials wishing to emphasize the arbitrary nature of the bargaining process often point to cases lost or won against all expectation (and the apparent merits of the case).
22. The more general issue of delay within procedure is discussed in the following chapter.
23. It is possible that the conduct of domestic negotiations by a powerless subordinate, authorized to receive but not offer concessions, may be

part of a deliberate tactic of 'calculated incompetence' (Walton and McKersie, *A Behavioral Theory of Labor Negotiations*, p. 68); by this means the union may be induced to reveal and perhaps compromise its hand, while management's position is safeguarded. It is impossible to determine whether this is often a deliberate strategy within engineering procedure; one might expect not, since unions would rapidly recognize this and retaliate.

24. The importance of management's internal politics has been further explored by N. W. Chamberlain and J. W. Kuhn, *Collective Bargaining*, McGraw-Hill, 1965 edn., Ch. 9. It might be added that an industrial relations manager may be assisted in intra-organizational bargaining even more by unconstitutional sanctions (actual or potential) than by resolute union use of procedure.
25. See E. Goffman, *Encounters*, Bobbs-Merrill, 1961.
26. This distinction is made by A. Douglas, *Industrial Peacemaking*, Columbia University Press, 1962, pp. 15–18.
27. For this reason, it is possible to overstress the argument that procedure allows domestic negotiators to 'pass the buck' and that these should be obliged to 'live with their own mistakes'. Confrontation situations abound in which compromise is made possible only by the introduction of some face-saving mechanism, usually from outside.
28. Douglas, op. cit., p. 163.
29. The general importance of such shared understandings was emphasized by J. T. Dunlop, *Industrial Relations Systems*, Holt, 1958; this analysis has been applied in the context of British engineering by Marsh.
30. This may be compared with American experience: 'shop grievances appear in conventionalized forms appropriate to the particular agreement in force' (J. W. Kuhn, *Bargaining in Grievance Settlement*, p. 11). It is also interesting to consider Gouldner's account of the 'displacement' of a grievance concerning managerial authority into a wage demand. The latter proved more readily resoluble, not least because 'in a sense, a wage demand is always legitimate, and it is only a question of "how much?" ' (A. W. Gouldner, *Wildcat Strike*, Routledge and Kegan Paul, 1955). This argument should not of course be overstressed: even pay demands have 'qualitative', implications. A firm may feel unable to concede a particular claim, for example, without jeopardizing its whole pay structure.
31. *Written Evidence*, para. 24. See also paras. 194–6.
32. Government Social Survey, *Workplace Industrial Relations*, 1968, pp. 35, 66. The percentage of full-time officers and shop stewards considering unconstitutional action justified in certain circumstances was as follows:

	Officers	Stewards
(a) if management has broken an agreement	62	77
(b) if management appears to be resorting to unreasonable delay in dealing with grievances	67	70
(c) if there is no other way of preventing management from discharging one of their workmates unfairly	73	78

(d) in any situation where they think that by acting in this way they can get what they want	11	23

33. *Report*, 1960, p. 127.
34. Such a situation arose in one of the cases studied: the personnel department was determined that the company should prove to an employee group its refusal to 'surrender to blackmail'; but once a strike occurred, concessions were forced by other managers unwilling to face the short-term losses of production.
35. EEF, *Written Evidence*, para. 18.
36. R. Dubin, *Working Union-Management Relations*, Prentice-Hall 1958, pp. 208–9.
37. W. E. J. McCarthy and S. R. Parker, *Shop Stewards and Workshop Relations*, Royal Commission Research Paper 10, H.M.S.O., 1968, p. 55.
38. Marsh and McCarthy, *Disputes Procedures in Britain*, p. 19; emphasis in original.
39. See J. E. T. Eldridge, *Industrial Disputes*, Routledge and Kegan Paul, 1968, p. 70.
40. The issue of 'managerial functions' is discussed in more detail in the following chapter.
41. See above, n. 32.

6

Problems and Perspectives

This final chapter considers various aspects of engineering procedure which have often been the subject of controversy, and also discusses briefly the implications of proposed procedural reforms.

As was noted at the outset of this study, the engineering disputes procedure is unenviably prominent in the number and variety of its critics. The EEF, as creator of the system, has in turn been vigorous in its defence: thus the Federation's Director-General has argued that

> some of the Procedure's critics base their judgment on an incomplete or prejudiced assessment of the facts. The seemingly automatic and almost mechanical repetition of these criticisms has lent them a weight which far exceeds their merits.[1]

Such a characterization cannot, however, be easily applied to the comprehensive indictment of the Donovan Report:

> The engineering industry's disputes procedure must bear a large share of the responsibility for the failure of federated undertakings to devise adequate wage structures and for their inability to solve disputes over other issues in a constitutional manner. The procedure functions slowly. It hampers the development of well-designed pay structures by allowing sectional claims to be pursued right through to 'central conference' regardless of their implications for other workers in the same factory. It discourages effective company personnel policies because companies have no place in the agreed procedure, unresolved disputes in individual factories being referred to local conference and not to the company. It provides no general guidance on dealing with issues of discipline, redundancy and work practices and it is not well equipped to handle individual disputes on these topics, which, it implies, fall within

> the prerogative of employers 'to manage their own establishments', despite the obvious impossibility of fixing clear and immutable limits for such a prerogative.[2]

To evaluate this critique, three problems—delay, managerial prerogatives, and effectiveness—will be considered in detail. The remaining points can be discussed more briefly.

A central theme developed by the Royal Commission is its diagnosis of the 'fragmented' nature of the engineering industry procedure as an obstacle to an incomes policy. This consideration is beyond the purview of the present study, which is concerned primarily with the operation of procedure as a means of dispute resolution, rather than with an evaluation of the content of settlements against incomes-policy criteria.

Two minor though related issues are relevant to the present analysis. First, the *ad hoc* nature of procedural discussion may prevent consideration of a particular question in the context of a perhaps intricate pattern of domestic industrial relations. Moreover, references which involve obvious issues of general principle must needs be considered 'on their merits' in isolation.[3] As was shown in the previous chapter, formal procedure cannot easily accommodate references which lack a high degree of specificity: wider-ranging discussion is likely to occur in informal conferences. While the growing use of such informal channels reflects the pragmatism which has always characterized the application of engineering procedure, the need for such a mechanism can be interpreted as an indication of a remediable shortcoming in formal procedure as such.

A second element in the Donovan argument relates to the ambivalent status in procedure of the national multi-establishment company. While it seems logical that the structure of the EEF should accommodate itself to the existence of such companies, it is not altogether evident that the district structure of Federation membership and disputes handling is the primary cause of any absence of comprehensive personnel policy within national companies.

Certainly the structure of the Federation does not *encourage* such developments, and may be an added inhibition to policy co-ordination in such firms. But it must also be noted that even firms with several establishments in the same district often show little evidence of co-ordination: while those few national companies attempting to apply a comprehensive industrial relations policy have not, apparently, found Federation structure a serious obstacle. Given the flexibility allowed to federated firms in developing domestic procedures, it is not obvious that external company representatives could not by mutual agreement be integrated into engineering procedure at this level. The present study certainly provided evidence that in external procedure company-wide comparisons and references to company-wide policy are not considered out of order.

More positively, it might be argued in favour of the existing arrangement that, given the frequency with which appeals are made to district comparisons, it permits such arguments to be readily validated and facilitates some degree of district uniformity. Moreover, 'localism' creates the regular interaction of officials on both sides which, it was suggested in the previous chapter, may facilitate the resolution of disputes. Finally, the argument of the CBI possesses some cogency:

> In the case of federated multi-plant firms we see little advantage in their setting up company procedures beyond establishment level. The role for the company lies much more in the field of laying down a sound industrial relations policy for the company as a whole and in providing advice on that policy at establishment level, not in direct intervention in the procedures.[4]

Delay

The Royal Commission view that 'the procedure functions slowly' is widely accepted. Marsh and Jones found that

> the time taken in processing issues to York in 1959 appears, measured from the first formal Works Conference to Central Conference itself, to have been about thirteen weeks on the average . . . Delay between Works and Local level was, on the average,

about six weeks, despite the fact that the Agreement lays down seven working days as a proper interval, 'unless otherwise mutually agreed upon.'[5]

The median delay between Works and Central was eleven weeks, the average being raised by a minority of cases involving disproportionate delays. More recently, Marsh and McCarthy have suggested that 'there is no evidence that procedural delays have grown substantially since 1959, but on the evidence available it can be said that engineering compares unfavourably with . . . other industries . . .'[6]

Twenty of the thirty-three cases in the present study involved adult manual workers: only four proceeded to Central Conference. Of this small sample, delay between Works and Central Conferences was ten weeks on average. Eleven of the twenty references were discussed at Local Conference; the average delay between the two external stages was 3½ weeks—little more than half the time reported by Marsh and Jones for their sample of Central Conference references in 1959. The average delay between Works and Local levels, in the case of the four references which reached York, was less than a fortnight; this might suggest that at least some Central Conference references are recognized at an early stage as particularly urgent or 'difficult', and are handled with special expedition. If the cases studied are at all representative of the general functioning of procedure in the Coventry district, they would appear to suggest that in terms of speed the local operation is unusually efficient.

Trade unionists are apt to attribute procedural delay in engineering either to employer prevarication or to the structure of procedure itself. The EEF by contrast has argued that criticisms of delay

> are either ill-informed or come from those who would prefer to be free to take industrial action first and discuss the alleged grievance later. While undue delay is inexcusable, account must be taken of the need to give time for the proper administration of the procedure. Even if central conferences could be held once every week, both parties at nearly all levels would require time to prepare their cases, make the necessary investigations and

> collect the evidence they think they need and arrange for the proper handling of the case at each stage of the procedure, so that it would be unlikely that the average period of a claim from domestic discussions to central conference would be very much less than at present.[7]

The Federation's Director-General has added that 'we feel that an important contributory factor to delay is the inadequate number of trade union officials available at local level to deal with claims and disputes.'[8] Marsh and Jones concur at least in part with this interpretation: 'It seems fair to suggest that since most references come from the unions, it is their machinery which is mainly responsible for procedural delays outside the work-place.'[9]

Causes of delay would seem to fall into three main categories. The first type is inherent in the administration of procedure itself. Since Central Conferences are held monthly, and a reference must be received at least a fortnight in advance, there is a built-in delay of two to six weeks at this stage—essential, according to the Federation's argument above, to allow each side to prepare its case. At the earlier stages of procedure, some time must normally elapse between an application for a conference and a date acceptable to all the parties. With the thirty-three cases studied, Works and Local Conferences were held on average some 2½ weeks after the union's application. It is this delay which the Federation attributes primarily to a shortage of trade-union officials; yet this interpretation does not appear wholly adequate. The experience of the present writer was that meetings could be arranged with local union officers at short notice, providing a sufficient choice of dates and times was offered. The problem arises when a conference date must be arranged mutually convenient for company industrial relations managers and union and Employers' Association officials, *all* of whom have crowded diaries.

The second category of delay arises between failure to agree at one level of procedure and application for a conference at the next. Since most references are union-initiated, this commonly reflects the operation (at times cumbersome) of union machinery. This can be particularly apparent in the case of reference to Central Conference, which must be made at National Executive level, and requires the prior consideration of a detailed report from the district concerned. At local level, a reference may on occasion 'get lost' within a union's administrative processes after failure to agree at Works: it is unusual for a Local Conference to be requested on the spot, and a full-time official may sometimes forget the existence of a reference unless prodded by the workers involved. And at any stage of procedure, delay in processing a reference further may reflect indecision as to whether and how the claim should be pursued.

The third source of procedural delay is inherent in the bargaining process. In some cases, the existence of further stages of procedure may itself inhibit speedy settlement—through fear that whatever is offered in the early stages will be rejected, making further concessions necessary. In so far as Central Conference has lost much of its former mystique, and is treated as just another stage of procedure, such tactical delay is inevitably compounded. Occasionally there is evidence that a union refrains from pursuing a claim when its bargaining position appears temporarily weak, only to revive it when circumstances appear more propitious. Probably more often, delay is a consequence of informal bargaining activity. Despite a formal outcome of failure to agree, a conference may offer some suggestion of a possible basis for agreement; or a conference may be adjourned to allow a potential solution to be explored (if no settlement is reached in such circumstances, a retrospective failure to agree can normally be registered). Unless such extra-procedural exchanges prove fruitless, further reference through procedure will be suspended.

The argument that procedural delays are excessive may involve either (or both) of the following propositions. First it may be suggested that the time between the various levels of procedure could be reduced without unreasonably affecting the quality of decision-making—or interfering with the opportunities for informal negotiation. The present study offers no basis for evaluating this claim. Second, it may be argued that procedure is unnecessarily long—and more specifically, that the value of Central Conference does not justify the time required to complete this stage. Such an assertion implies a judgment of the *effectiveness* of the different levels of procedure—which will be considered below.

What can be suggested with some confidence is that the delays (at times protracted) involved in procedure—or at least, in the minority of references which reach the higher stages—adversely affect its acceptability. Lack of urgency on the part of one side may be viewed by the other, justifiably or otherwise, as intentional and tactical. In particular, union officials—while perhaps accepting that delay is sometimes valuable in reducing passions and allowing detailed thought—commonly argue that procedural delay can cause more anger and frustration than the original dispute. The view seems widespread that union members would be more willing to observe the requirements of procedure were the time involved reduced.

A particular problem results from the absence of any formal selectivity in the functioning of procedure. While urgent cases do appear to be processed more speedily than most others, even the minimum delay inherent in procedure may be excessive with many 'perishable' issues. For example an employee whose dismissal is contested is likely to have found another job before procedure is exhausted; in any case, his fellow workers cannot normally be expected to apply sanctions on his behalf several weeks after the event. This fact has been candidly recognized by one local employers' representative:

> our experience in referring dismissal questions to the procedure is that whilst it provides the union with a formal opportunity to ventilate a grievance, such discussions seldom alter the material outcome of the cases in question. The procedure is nevertheless valuable in removing the pressure of industrial action.

The problem of perishable issues is clearly aggravated by the 'managerial functions' provision in the procedure agreement. Were the *status quo* to apply in such cases, the unions would have less obvious cause for complaint; though it is the employers' contention that under such circumstances *they* would find the delays intolerable. This factor leads naturally to a consideration of the whole issue of managerial prerogatives.

Managerial Prerogatives

The origins of engineering procedure—in employer victories in the national lock-outs of 1897–8 and 1922—are reflected in the incorporation of specific defences of managerial prerogatives; or, as trade unionists would tend to argue, the institutionalization of 'managerial bias'. The characteristics which provide much of the uniqueness of engineering procedure are the structure of 'employer conciliation' and the 'managerial functions' provision.

The term 'employer conciliation' has been devised by Marsh to denote the fact that under the provision for avoiding disputes, the Chairman is at all stages a representative of the company, while at Local and Central Conferences the case is argued before a panel of employers. It is scarcely surprising that this sytem is viewed in trade-union circles as a mechanism whereby

> union representatives are forced to appeal to other employers in an industry in order to see that justice is done; thus the unions appear as supplicants and the employers as judge and jury in their own cause.[10]

Marsh suggests however that unions do not, 'despite their protests in principle about "employer conciliation" . . . find this particularly prejudicial in practice'.[11]

It has been shown previously that one feature of Local Conferences in the Coventry district is the reduction of the employer's panel to something of a formality. Usually it comprises only two local employers, and it is not expected that these should participate in formal conference proceedings (which are handled by the Chairman—either the

Association Director or his Deputy). Whatever its historical origins, the role of the panel in Coventry today is essentially advisory and conciliatory, and is exercised in adjournment discussion. Officials of the Association argue that the support of practising managers can be of great value should they wish to persuade a company that its position is unwise or unreasonable; and that their presence can aid the consideration of the implications of a particular claim and the possible settlements. From the conferences attended, it was not evident that the panel's contribution is typically of great importance (given the experience and influence of Association officials in their own right); but employers themselves seem to value the opportunity to participate in this way (perhaps in part because this allows them to 'keep an eye' on their own trade-union representatives).

The wider argument of employer bias is contested by Association officials who act as Chairmen at Works or Local Conferences. They commonly assert that some of their toughest arguments take place during adjournments, with company representatives: often, they suggest, they argue the union case better than the union officer himself.[12] Where this does occur, it is of course private from the union side, to whom the Chairman appears solely in his role as employer spokesman. And while conferences certainly do occur in which he attempts to indicate the advantages of a more conciliatory approach, the evidence does not suggest that these are particularly typical. Moreover, other conferences may have the traditional function of reinforcing the company's resistance to a union demand.

This is not to deny that the Chairman may often exercise a 'boundary role' which parallels that of the union official[13] and aids the process of compromise. At other times, while not actually pressing for specific concessions, he may act as a 'candid friend' and induce a self-critical approach in a company which has reacted over-defensively to a union proposal. But it remains true that the Chairman is obliged to perform simultaneously two roles—as representative and mediator—which may at times be in conflict.

In general, this role conflict is handled with skill and accomplishment; yet it is questionable how far one individual can invariably act effectively both as 'neutral' chairman and as spokesman for one protagonist—and the handling of the occasional dispute may suffer in consequence.

Managerial Functions

The 'managerial functions' clause (II (1) (d) of the procedure) prescribes that—with the exception of certain questions specifically excluded—a company may introduce changes in working conditions, and that such changes shall stand despite any union objection pending the operation of procedure.[14]

While this aspect of the procedure agreement has always aroused intense resentment among trade unionists, it is commonly argued that in practice the absence of any blanket *status quo* provisions has very limited consequences for the conduct of the industrial relations in engineering. The EEF has itself emphasized that area of topics from which the doctrine of managerial functions is excluded:

> One of the paradoxes of relations in the Engineering Industry is that the Federation has probably gone further than any other employers' organization in the provision of clauses which provide for the maintenance of the status quo pending negotiations on proposed changes in conditions, yet finds itself open to more pressure on this score than any other industry.[15]

And Marsh has stated that in those areas where the principle of managerial functions clearly does apply,

> engineering employers, having asserted their rights to the utmost on two major national occasions, have, in practice, been prepared to relax the operation of these rights to meet the force of circumstances. Managerial functions has become a defensive slogan rather than a reality in all but a small number of cases.[16]

Continuing union hostility is interpreted as opposition to the symbol rather than the reality of this aspect of engineering procedure: 'an issue of history and pride, rather than practice.'[17]

Clearly, engineering procedure does indeed specify

major areas in which the principle of *status quo* applies—though it might be noted that these include, in effect, the whole field within which *trade unions* pursue changes. Perhaps of even greater practical importance, the rights formally assigned to managements under the national agreement are of very limited value in a period of relatively full employment and in the face of strong and extensive shop-floor union organization. A wide range of alterations in workshop practices can in reality be affected only by mutual consent; and the more powerful and self-assured the workers' organization within the factory, the wider this range is likely to be.

In consequence, the principle of the *status quo* may operate even where the doctrine of managerial functions in theory applies. A company which is unable to obtain employee co-operation in an alteration will commonly refrain from exercising its formal rights for fear of provoking a stoppage or other sanctions. The company itself may initiate a reference in procedure (or, more often, at an informal conference) in the hope that the full-time union official may assist in obtaining his members' compliance. Yet it can scarcely be argued that such restraint is universal. It is the readiness of union members to take action (in breach of procedure) in each situation which sets the practical limits of managerial prerogatives; and this readiness will naturally vary (and not always, it may be supposed, in ratio to the merits of each particular case). In the dismissal case (number 20) covered by the present study, management's firmness was no doubt related to its assessment that industrial action in support of the employee concerned was improbable. At a more general level, it should be remembered that the Coventry district has been far from typical in the tightness of the labour market and the strength and self-assurance of trade unionism at the point of production; there may well be other areas in which the practical consequences of the managerial functions clause are greater.

Effectiveness

The most manifest criterion of procedural effectiveness is the 'disposal rate' of references: the proportion which achieve some form of resolution at each level. Table III showed that of manual worker references from all districts, between 4 and 6 per cent have ended in failure to agree at York in recent years. For Coventry references, the proportion has tended to be somewhat higher. More staff references exhaust procedure without resolution—in some years, considerably more: and again, the proportion of Coventry staff references unresolved has in the majority of recent years been above the national average. Disposal rates for staff and manual references alike were lower in the 1960s than previously. A further point often noted is the tendency for the disposal rate to fall as references move up the procedure—though as Table X indicates, this tendency can easily be exaggerated.

TABLE X

Disposal Rates[18] of Manual and Staff References, Coventry and National, 1963–9 (in Percentages)

	COVENTRY			NATIONAL		
	Works	*Local*	*Central*	*Works*	*Local*	*Central*
MANUAL						
1963	74	38	73	78	55	57
1964	67	62	48	76	58	53
1965	58	61	71	74	58	58
1966	61	61	61	73	50	54
1967	69	57	46	76	59	49
1968	64	64	64	73	53	61
1969	63	42	64	76	52	63
Average	65	55	61	75	55	56
STAFF						
1963	31	72	57	71	57	47
1964	45	34	74	66	57	50
1965	31	60	44	64	64	50
1966	22	12	35	46	42	26
1967	69	48	36	63	41	40
1968	58	73	11	68	51	44
1969	48	42	41	67	50	41
Average	43	49	43	64	52	43

Nationally, in recent years, disposal rates at Works level have been significantly above those at the higher levels of procedure. But the contrast *between* the two highest levels is far less marked; indeed, because of the different basis of calculation it is difficult to argue, on the evidence of disposal rates alone, that Central Conference is any less effective than Local. In the Coventry district, any generalization regarding the relative effectiveness of the different stages is even more dangerous. Disposal rates have fluctuated sharply in recent years, and have tended to be higher at Central Conference, and lower at Works level, than the national average. The explanation for these differences is not readily apparent.

The formal outcome of references is in any case not necessarily a satisfactory index of procedural effectiveness. As Marsh and McCarthy have indicated,

> disposal does not always entail a positive and clear settlement. Moreover, it is not merely that disposal rates are relatively low at Central Conference. It is that the majority of issues which are disposed of at this level are not settled in the sense that an agreement is reached; they are mostly sent back in some form for ultimate settlement in the establishment from which they came . . . Most issues in which a failure to agree is avoided are not settled between the two sides at York. Rather are they referred back, or retained in the hands of Central Conference pending further inquiries or action. In most instances this latter course also results in a case either being abandoned or returned for ultimate settlement to the establishment where it originated. Thus in 1966, for example, only some 10 per cent of all cases disposed of were actually settled at Central Conference, and many of these were formal acknowledgments of settlements already arrived at domestically.[19]

Conversely, an outcome in failure to agree may also be misleading (one reason, perhaps, why the term is not officially used at Central Conference level). Given that the majority of references concern wage issues, a failure to agree may on occasion be highly 'successful' inasmuch as it may persuade one party of the determination of the other.

The small proportion of clear-cut settlements at Central

Conference—which to some extent reflects the inability of the central authorities to *impose* a settlement on the parties (who are absent from the formal proceedings)—is one reason for the particular criticism which has been directed at this stage of the procedure. The President of the AEF, for example, has characterized York as a 'cowards' castle':

> managements are either refusing or we are progressing matters to Central Conference in the hope, either that management will be given protection or we might get something a little better than we are able to establish in local negotiations.[20]

This echoes the opinion of Marsh and McCarthy that

> the overwhelming majority of cases considered here do not involve matters which it is normal to settle by centralized decision-making between the parties. They are, in fact, simply workplace issues *which happen not to have been resolved at the level at which it is most appropriate that this should have been decided.*[21]

The view that the very existence of Central Conference can inhibit earlier settlement, since the parties know that failure to agree locally will not be 'the end of the road', is widely held in Coventry, and is certainly not confined to the unions. The argument is in essence that where a settlement is achieved at York this is in most cases *simply because York is the final stage of procedure,* rather than because the reference requires the special qualities of national negotiators; there is thus little justification for the delay inherent in the Central stage. It would appear from recent national negotiations that the EEF itself now concedes that such a stage may reasonably be dispensed with, except for the interpretation of national agreements.

The bulk of references in external procedure do not of course reach Central Conference; but for these too, the concept of settlement may be somewhat ambiguous. Table XI indicates certain outcomes of Coventry references in the years 1965–9. This shows that some 30 to 40 per cent of conferences result in a formal settlement within procedure at Works or Local level, while 10 to 25 per cent of the references proceed to Central Conference. However, almost half the cases in most recent years are neither formally resolved in the earlier stages of procedure nor referred to Central Conference. Accordingly, these are either adjourned or referred back for further domestic discussion, settled informally, or else allowed to drop.[22] And as was noted above, a similar proportion of cases at York result in similar treatment.

TABLE XI

Certain Outcomes of Coventry References, 1965–9

	1965	*1966*	*1967*	*1968*	*1969*
Works Conferences	341	292	351	359	404
Settled, Works and Local	114 (33%)	105 (36%)	126 (36%)	149 (42%)	134 (33%)
Central Conferences	65 (19%)	73 (25%)	49 (14%)	45 (13%)	95 (23%)

These figures might be interpreted as indicative of the high degree of flexibility and informality which surrounds the operation of formal procedure. Experience in both Britain and America has shown that the formal processing of issues through procedure is intimately connected with the far less formal aspects of bargaining; the use of procedure may provide the arena for off-the-record dealing, may be a bargaining gambit, or may provide a substitute for settling issues.[23] Such flexibility might be particularly necessary in the context of British engineering. Formal substantive regulation has traditionally been restricted in application: to a large extent, conditions within the workplace have been determined by more or less informal domestic agreements and understandings, reflecting the real balance of power on the shop floor, and often sanctified under the title of 'custom and practice'. Of necessity, the link between the complex system of domestic regulation and the external institutions of trade union and employers' association must be in practice flexible, whatever the formal provisions of procedure may prescribe.[24]

The conclusions of the present writer are that engineering procedure does to a large extent satisfy the requirements of all the parties in the Coventry area (where strong union organization in the factory helps to shape its operation). Yet this is so precisely because the parties have considerable choice as to whether or not a particular issue is referred to external procedure, and whether they continue to pursue it procedurally in the absence of early settlement. The option of alternative forms of treatment entails that those references which do enter procedure are to an important extent pre-selected; while the fact that extra-procedural or even unconstitutional means are in practice open must needs profoundly influence the conduct of discussions *within* procedure.

The Future of Engineering Procedure

Trade-union pressure for major revision of engineering procedure, which accumulated in the immediate post-war period, largely subsided after the minor amendments agreed in 1955. The recent detailed negotiations, initiated by a Special Conferencc in April 1969, reflect a revival of union aspirations, the impact of such detached critics as the Royal Commission, and an unprecedented readiness on the part of the EEF to accept a wholesale restructuring of procedure.

By the end of 1970 a broad area of agreement appeared to have been achieved. The most significant of the proposed changes may be summarized under three headings.

First, the purely *ad hoc* nature of existing procedure would be altered. At national level, an Industrial Relations Council would be established; while within individual establishments, Joint Works Committees representative of management and all unions could be created. (The existing procedure does indeed authorize the formation of Works Committees; but these, at least in the form prescribed, are virtually non-existent.) The consideration by the JWC of a question arising would substitute for the existing Works Conference.

Second, the principle of managerial functions would be limited to circumstances 'where an employer takes a decision which is within the framework of an existing agreement or an established practice'. At the same time, a broadened area would be specified in which the *status quo* would be prescribed. There would however remain a 'grey area' not unambiguously covered by either formulation.

Third, procedure would be shortened to permit the speedier handling of disputes. As already noted, the operation of a JWC would remove the necessity for a Works conference; and Central Conferences would not be held, except to resolve disputes concerning the interpretation or application of national agreements.

Despite this substantial area of agreement, negotiations reached deadlock in the first half of 1971, after union efforts to remove the remaining ambiguities involving 'managerial functions' by extending an effective *status quo* arrangement to the 'grey area' noted above. Failing satisfaction, threats were made on several occasions (particularly by the Amalgamated Union of Engineering Workers) to withdraw from the existing procedure agreement.

At the time of writing it is unclear whether all the unions concerned will indeed withdraw, leaving the industry without a disputes procedure. Should this happen, it seems inconceivable that some form of procedural arrangements will not continue to operate informally, leading eventually to a new procedure agreement. And given the fairly narrow margin of difference between the EEF and the unions, it would be surprising if such agreement were not along lines broadly similar to those described above. While there is little to be gained, given the present uncertainty, from any detailed attempt at the prediction of the consequences of such procedural revision, certain tentative assessments may be suggested.

While reforms of this nature would not meet all the most widely voiced criticisms of the existing procedure, they would appear relevant to several features which are commonly held to constitute serious problems. A new agreement would presumably prove markedly more acceptable within the industry than is the case with the current procedure: first because its more streamlined character ought to permit a considerable reduction in delays; second because of the alterations to the managerial functions clause (even though the practical effect of a revised formulation might well be somewhat limited); and third, and most important, because the arrangements would be accepted voluntarily. And certainly, those union members and officials who resent the existing procedure as much for its origins as its content would experience a greater obligation to observe a freshly negotiated structure. In addition, the operation of a system of JWCs would almost inevitably reduce the fragmentation of claims which is facilitated by the present procedure: a development which, judging from a number of the references investigated in the course of the present study, would be of major benefit to many companies.

Beyond this, the opinions of those involved in industrial relations in engineering differ in evaluating the probable consequences of procedural revision. In part, this is because many of the details of a new procedure remain to be formulated; the exact functioning of the revised Local Conference, for example—in most cases the first and last formal involvement of the outside officials—remains unclear. In part also, this is because any such prediction enters the realm of conjecture. It is reasonable to suppose that in many respects the conference would be transformed: presumably it would no longer be a major goal to manoeuvre the desired presentation of a case onto the notes; rather, serious negotiation would of necessity become central. An increase in the length of conferences, and the number of adjournments, might also be expected—the exchanges which can at present extend over several meetings becoming, in effect, compressed into a single conference. For similar reasons, a considerable elaboration would presumably be necessary of the existing rudimentary pre-conference communication between the domestic parties and their outside representatives.

It is also reasonable to assume that pressures towards domestic resolution of questions arising would be far stronger than at present: with only one external stage of procedure, inhibitions against recourse to this stage could well be intense. Conceivably, the composition of references to external procedure would be transformed in consequence: if routine domestic resolution of straightforward bargaining issues were to become almost invariably the norm, Local Conference could possibly come to represent a forum for more complex questions. This would almost certainly require that the revised Local Conference function in a manner which avoids deterring, as at present, the reference of such problems to formal procedure.

It might also be expected that the reduced opportunities, within formal procedure, for temporization could result in an escalation of the already considerable volume of informal and quasi-procedural activity. Any psychological inhibition on reference to Local Conference would enhance the attraction of the informal conference with trade union and Association officials. Their more or less open involvement while negotiations remain nominally at domestic level might also be anticipated. Parallel informal processes could be expected after the exhaustion of procedure; and indeed, it would scarcely be surprising were the Local Conference to develop the artillery of temporizing devices at present employed at York.

The existing procedure, in brief, serves in some ways to encourage unconstitutional action, while—in part through a process of attrition—discouraging constitutional sanctions. A revised procedure could conceivably bring a significant reduction in unconstitutional outbreaks; at the same time, the pressure for constitutional resolution of claims within the domestic setting would be far greater, and the role of domestic procedure as a basis for bargaining against the background of power relationships might well become even more manifest than at present. In addition, procedure could be far more rapidly exhausted; but where a stoppage is not seriously desired by either side, informal means would undoubtedly emerge for prolonging the bargaining process.

A final comment is necessitated by the Industrial Relations Act (IRA) of 1971. The introduction of this legislation itself interrupted negotiations on the revision of the engineering procedure, the unions insisting that the new agreement should explicitly exclude any possibility of being held legally binding. And while this demand was eventually conceded by the EEF, the climate engendered by the government's action could well have contributed to the breakdown in negotiations.

Even assuming that a new procedure is eventually agreed, its operation could be seriously affected by the new legislation. It has been seen that effective dispute handling depends on a delicate and flexible interaction of formal and informal processes, against the background of the common but tacit understandings of the parties; and that a revised procedure would almost certainly require a further elaboration of such informal processes. It has also been seen that the possibility of unconstitutional sanctions is an indispensable element in effective domestic bargaining. Under the IRA, however, such sanctions are defined as 'unfair industrial practices' and constitute grounds for action in the courts.

For a management to attempt to enforce its new legal 'rights' would plainly disrupt the delicate structure of domestic industrial relations. (The mind boggles at the havoc which would ensue if the machinery of the IRA were used to impose legally binding procedure agreements within individual companies.) The very *possibility* of actions which are a normal part of industrial relations in engineering giving rise to litigation will probably render the parties' mutual expectations, for a time at least, highly uncertain. The whole basis of informal relationships which underlie successful dispute resolution could well be jeopardized.[25]

REFERENCES

1. Proceedings of a Special Conference between the Engineering Employers' Federation and the Confederation of Shipbuilding and Engineering Unions, 16 April 1970, pp. 2—3.
2. Royal Commission on Trade Unions and Employers' Associations, *Report*, Cmnd. 3623, 1968, p. 106. For the EEF reply to these other criticisms see *The Donovan Report: an Assessment*, 1969.
3. In fact, though all settlements are officially 'without precedent" managements throughout the study showed themselves extremely conscious of the wider implications and potential repercussions of references. It is of course always open to a company to refuse any concession to a sectional claim, while offering to hold domestic discussions of the issue on a comprehensive basis (as indeed occurred in several of the cases studied); such discussions can and often do involve outside officials.
4. Confederation of British Industry, *Disputes Procedures*, 1970, p. 13.
5. 'Engineering Procedure', *British Journal of Industrial Relations*, 1964, pp. 242–3.
6. *Disputes Procedures in Britain*, p. 22.
7. *Written Evidence*, para. 175.
8. Proceedings of the Special Conference, p. 4.
9. 'Engineering Procedure', *British Journal of Industrial Relations*, 1964, p. 244.
10. Marsh and McCarthy, *Disputes Procedures*, p. 17.
11. *Industrial Relations in Engineering*, p. 119.
12. A colourful argument that Association representatives typically support the union position—not on its merits but in order to avoid possible industrial conflict—was presented to the Royal Commission in the *Written Evidence* of Philips Industries. The Company stated (para. 17): 'We now find that more and more pressure is exerted upon us as a company, frequently with scant regard for reality, to make some concession to avoid "breaking the industrial peace", and this pressure comes not from the unions, but from fellow employers. We are now convinced that the machinery, although effective in some directions, is more an appeasement policy than a procedure for the avoidance of disputes'. They added (para. 19): 'We should like to comment that the working of the Procedure sometimes resembles a ritualistic death dance, in that most of the actual discussion takes place between professionals on either side who are more interested in the Procedure than the purpose for which it was established'.

    The typicality of this state of affairs is doubtful, if only because of the frequency with which conferences do result in failure to agree.
13. See above, p. 52
14. The relevant section of the procedure agreement is as follows:

    PROCEDURE FOR DEALING WITH QUESTIONS ARISING

    1a. The procedure of the Provisions for Avoiding Disputes so far as appropriate, applies to:—

(i) General alterations in wages;
(ii) Alterations in working conditions which are the subject of agreements officially entered into;
(iii) Alterations in the general working week;
but such alterations shall not be given effect to until the appropriate procedure between the Federation and the Trade Union or Unions concerned has been exhausted.

b. When the Management contemplates alterations in recognized working conditions which do not involve a change in material, means or method, and would result in work currently done by one class of workpeople in future being done by another class of workpeople in the establishment, the Management shall give the workpeople directly concerned or their representatives in the shop intimation of the intention, and afford an opportunity for discussion with a deputation of the workpeople concerned and/or their representatives in the shop. In the event of no settlement being reached, the Procedure outlined in Section (2)—Provisions for Avoiding Disputes—shall be operated.
The alterations concerned shall not be implemented until settlement has been reached or until the Procedure has been exhausted.
Where a contemplated alteration involves a change in the material, means or method and may result in one class of workpeople being replaced by another in the establishment, the Management shall as soon as possible notify their proposals to the workpeople directly concerned and/or their representative in the shop in order that there may be consultation between the parties concerned with a view to reaching agreement. If agreement is not achieved the workers concerned may give notice of an apprehended dispute, in which case the Management will not operate the proposed change for seven working days. The matter may be dealt with in accordance with the Provisions for Avoiding Disputes, the change being without prejudice to either party in any discussions which may take place.

c. Where any class of workpeople is displaced by reason of any act of the Management, consideration shall be given to the case of workpeople so displaced with a view, if practicable, of affording them in the establishment work suitable to their qualifications.

d. Questions arising which do not result in one class of workpeople being replaced by another in the establishment and on which discussion is desired, shall be dealt with in accordance with the Provisions for Avoiding Disputes and work shall proceed meantime under the conditions following the act of the Management.

15. *Written Evidence*, para. 161.
16. *Industrial Relations in Engineering*, p. 136.
17. Marsh and McCarthy, *Disputes Procedures*, p. 17.
18. Disposal rates have been calculated on the basis employed by Marsh and McCarthy, *Disputes Procedures*, Table 1, p. 20. The rate at Works level is calculated according to the formula $100 - \left(\frac{100\,L}{W}\right)$, where L is the number of Local Conferences in the year and W the number of Works Conferences. The rate at Local level is calculated on the same basis. At Central level the rate represents the number of Conferences not resulting in 'failure to agree'. It should be noted that since not all failures to agree at Works and Local level are pursued to the next stage of procedure, the rates shown are more generous than in the case of Central Conferences.
19. *Disputes Procedures*, p. 21. The EEF in reply argues (*The Donovan Report*, p. 34) that reference back is often necessary to allow the detailed domestic elaboration of a broad basis for compromise agreed nationally; and that it is often inappropriate to register formally the details of a settlement at Central Conference since these might be cited 'completely out of context' in support of other claims. These points perhaps cast doubt on the appropriateness of a national conference as the final stage in a disputes procedure.
20. *Proceedings of the Special Conference*, p. 12.
21. *Disputes Procedures*, p. 22; emphasis in original.
22. The outcomes of the 33 cases covered by the present study matched the above pattern closely.

23. See, for example, Kuhn, *Bargaining in Grievance Settlement.*
24. In this context it is worth citing the EEF response to the 'two systems' analysis of the Royal Commission (*The Donovan Report*, p. 10): 'the Federation's main objection to this diagnosis is the dramatic nature of the antithesis which is made between the formal and the informal systems'. This reaction is in line with the current disenchantment of industrial sociologists with the familiar analytical dichotomy between formal and informal organization. A simplistic counterposing of formal and informal does scant justice to the qualitative complexity of organizational relationships and diverts attention from their dynamic character; in most situations there exist emergent tendencies towards the structuring and formalization of 'informal' activities and relations, and also towards the intrusion of 'unofficial' or 'deviant' practices to supplement and modify what is formally prescribed. Relevant studies include W. H. Scott et al., *Technical Change and Industrial Relations*, Liverpool University Press, 1956, Appendix A; E. Wight Bakke, 'Concept of the Social Organization,' in M. Haire, *Modern Organization Theory*, Wiley, 1959; N. P. Mouzelis, *Organisation and Bureaucracy*, Routledge and Kegan Paul, 1967.
25. Cf. Marsh, *Disputes Procedures in Britain*, Royal Commission Research Paper 2, Part 1, H.M.S.O., 1966, p. 24, para. 104.

Appendix: the Case Studies

As part of this study, all the references entering Works Conference during a five-week period—33 cases in all—were investigated in detail. This Appendix presents an outline summary of the details of each case, while excluding some information in order to preserve anonymity. The format adopted is an introduction giving the background of each reference, then a description of the procedural discussions at each level and the eventual outcome. In most cases the issues raised are analyzed briefly. Attitudes and arguments are generally attributed merely to 'the union' or 'the company'. This is not to imply that the official position of the union, as expressed by its full-time official, is always identical with the views of its domestic members and representatives. Nor does it mean that the Employers' Association official, who as Chairman normally acts as company spokesman, does not approach some issues with a viewpoint different from that of the management representatives (or that the latter are themselves of one opinion). The intention is merely to illustrate the type of issues arising in procedure in the district, the type of arguments used, and the type of positions adopted; for this purpose, it is normally satisfactory to treat each party as a coherent entity. The implications of differences within each 'side' have been discussed previously.

The cases have been grouped according to subject-matter. The first twenty concern adult manual workers. Cases (1) to (7) are 'straight' pay claims for sections of time-rated workers; (8) to (10) involve questions of grading, though here too the effective goal is an increase in basic rates of pay; (11) to (15) relate to payment-by-results issues, while (16) concerns a productivity bonus. Then follow two 'miscellaneous' references with monetary implications. Cases (19) and (20) concern, respectively, manning and dismissal.

The next four references involve apprentices and junior workers; all concern matters arising from a national agreement concluded shortly before the research commenced.

Finally there are nine staff references. Cases (25) to (29) cover salaries; (30), hours of work; and (31) and (32), holiday arrangements. The final reference relates to redundancy.

Since one purpose of the individual studies is to illustrate the nature of references passing through procedure, it is reasonable to ask how representative they are of the distribution of cases over a longer period of time. One response might be that there is no such thing as a representative reference. An initially disconcerting feature of the study was the regularity with which those involved in a particular case would stress how untypical the specific issue was. But every reference possesses some unique features; and while it remains a live issue these features may well possess the greatest salience for those directly involved. The subject-matter of collective bargaining does not fall automatically into neat categories merely to suit the convenience of the researcher; all generalization entails a certain degree of violence to the complexity of raw reality. Yet fundamental similarities do exist; while any attempt to understand reality makes generalization inescapable.

A more specific problem is that even where it is possible to define a 'normal' pattern of references, this is by no means a constant pattern. As was seen previously, procedure displays large fluctuations from year to year in the number and outcome of references, and analogous variations occur in the composition of references. It is thus impossible to specify with any precision the standard against

TABLE XII

Outcome of Conferences (in Percentages)

		MANUAL			STAFF			TOTAL		
		1968	*1969*	*Sample*	*1968*	*1969*	*Sample*	*1968*	*1969*	*Sample*
WC:	Settled	35	28	15	21	23	11	31	27	14
	Adjourned	28	33	23	32	28	0	29	32	17
	FTA	37	38	61	46	49	89	39	42	69
	(N)	(281)	(308)	(26)	(108)	(138)	(9)	(389)	(446)	(35)
LC:	Settled	31	22	43	12	12	40	25	19	42
	Ref. back	3	4	0	10	2	0	5	3	0
	Adjourned	26	28	0	32	29	20	27	29	5
	FTA	41	45	57	46	57	40	42	49	53
	(N)	(101)	(113)	(14)	(41)	(65)	(5)	(142)	(178)	(16)
CC:	Settled	8	11	0	14	12	0	10	11	0
	RB/Retained	50	42	43	7	29	0	38	38	38
	Adjourned	0	11	0	7	0	0	2	7	0
	FTA	42	36	57	71	59	100	50	44	62
	(N)	(36)	(66)	(7)	(14)	(34)	(1)	(50)	(100)	(8)

which to measure the representativeness of a particular batch of cases.

As a rough basis for comparison, various aspects of the sample of 33 cases are matched against data for all local references in the two years 1968–69. Table XII shows the outcome of conferences at each stage of procedure; Table XIII, the subject of the references; Table XIV, the distribution by major companies; and Table XV, the distribution by unions.

From Table XII it can be seen that the total number of Works Conferences in the sample, and their distribution between manual and staff references, approximate closely to the pattern of previous years. However, the sample is notable for its low disposal rate: failure to agree at Works Conference being 70 per cent higher than in the previous years, and more Local and Central Conferences also ending in failure to agree. The proportion of Works Conferences in the sample ending in failure to agree at Central Conference was 14·3 per cent, compared with 6·4 per cent of all local Works Conferences in 1968 and 9·9 per cent in 1969. This might suggest that the references in the sample were in some sense unusually difficult. However, a higher than average proportion of all conferences in the sample ended in a clear-cut outcome (either formal settlement or failure to agree); this was particularly true of Local Conferences. In part this may be because Table XII, unlike the subsequent Tables, relates to hearings rather than references. A proportion of adjourned or referred

TABLE XIII

Subject of References (in Percentages)

	1968	*1969*	*Sample*
Wages	76	69	76
Conditions	7	7	3
Holidays	1	8	9
Discipline	4	2	3
Redundancy	3	3	3
Other	8	12	6
(N)	(358)	(400)	(33)

TABLE XIV

Distribution of References: Companies (in Percentages)

	1968	*1969*	*Sample*
3 largest firms	33	35	27
10 largest firms	62	69	73
(N)	(358)	(400)	(33)

TABLE XV

Distribution of References: Trade Unions (in Percentages)

	1968	*1969*	*Sample*
MANUAL:			
TGWU	75	72	67
AEF	68	72	46
Other	28*	37*	4
Joint Refs.	52	50	17
(N)	(263)	(282)	(24)
STAFF:			
ACTSS	25	15	11
CAWU	23	28	0
DATA	23	23	22
ASTMS (A)	15	16	11
ASTMS (1)	29	30	56
Joint Refs.	14	8	0
(N)	(95)	(118)	(9)

*These are spurious figures, representing the total appearances of up to ten smaller manual unions as a percentage of total references; in fact most of these appearances are in references also involving other minority unions. So between 80 and 90 per cent of references in a typical year involve only the two main unions (singly or jointly). The third ranking manual union in 1968 was involved in 11 per cent of references; in 1969, 9 per cent.

back references end in failure to agree at a resumed conference; analysis of references is thus likely to show a higher proportion of failures to agree than analysis of conferences. It is in any case necessary to bear in mind the extent to which disposal rates can fluctuate from year to year.

In terms of subject-matter, the sample matches the previous pattern closely. The proportion of 'conditions' and 'other issues' is somewhat lower than in most years; with so small a sample this is scarcely of statistical significance, but may reflect seasonal factors.[1] Though the proportion of pay claims is in line with past experience, its make-up may also reflect seasonal factors: reviews of staff salaries and day-workers' wages often occur at a particular time of year, and a number of disputes relating to such questions entered external procedure during the period of the study. A particular national agreement (on pay of apprentices and junior workers) also made its mark on the composition of the sample.

Because of the small number of references involved, no attempt is made to match their incidence at individual companies with the pattern of previous years. Table XIV does however compare the sample with the years 1968 and 1969 in terms of the combined involvement of the largest firms federated with the local Association. A close correspondence can be seen, suggesting that in this respect the sample is representative.

Finally, Table XV shows the incidence of references by trade unions. The most obvious divergence from the previous two years is the almost total monopoly of manual worker references by the two main unions, and the small number of joint references. It should be noted that both factors fluctuate markedly from year to year; at the same time, the characteristics of the sample cannot be attributed merely to chance variations. The involvement of the smaller unions and the incidence of joint references are related. Just under 15 per cent of manual trade unionists in the district are members of the smaller unions; but as was seen in a previous chapter, most of these societies are characterized by a reluctance to *initiate* references in procedure. For this reason, very few of the small sectional claims which predominate in procedure involve the minority unions; the latter are far more likely to appear in the minority of multi-union references which concern a whole factory or large department. Whereas the bulk of sectional references are claims by workers for some improvement, the larger multi-union references often relate to some change initiated by management. An obvious example is the introduction of a new model in motor vehicle manufacturing; a range of major issues (concerning piece rates, labour loading, track speeds, the introduction and manning of new machinery or processes, new shift arrangements, special transitional payments, etc.) may be referred to procedure by either management or the unions. Other changes initiated by management which commonly give rise to joint references in procedure include lay-offs and short-time working. It is also common for the negotiation of a new comprehensive agreement at national level to be followed by a series of multi-union references concerning its implementation in particular establishments.

While multi-union references are comparatively rare, they may involve up to ten separate organizations and hence have a disproportionate impact on statistics of union participation in procedure. Such references show some seasonal, and even stronger (and apparently random) month-to-month variation in incidence. The absence of any such reference (and the small number even of two-union references) in the sample is thus the principal factor underlying the divergence from the customary pattern of manual union involvement.

While white-collar references also vary in some respects from previous annual patterns, this may perhaps be attributed merely to the small sample size. It is also possible that the higher involvement of Division 1 of ASTMS (like the predominance of the TGWU in the manual sample) may be an accurate reflection of short-term trends in procedural usage.

In so far as it is possible to define a 'normal' pattern of procedural references, the 33 covered by the sample may thus be said to bear a tolerable though by no means exact correspondence to this pattern. The most important divergences noted are the absence of the type of broad issue involving a number of minority unions; and the relative inefficacy of procedure—particularly the early stages—in resolving the points at issue. But as a general illustration of the content of procedural discussions, the case studies may be considered to serve their purpose reasonably well.

1. 'To claim an increase for female cleaners'

This reference was a claim for a straightforward pay increase for female cleaners, employed as time-workers at one of the company's two local factories. (Since the case studies took place before decimalization, all references to money are in shillings and pence.)

Works. The union argued for an increase of 1s. an hour on two grounds: it was two years since the cleaners had last had an increase in wages, and during this period other day-workers had received two advances; and cleaners at the company's other factory had recently received an extra 9d. an hour. The company replied that the pay of this group of cleaners had been and remained among the highest in the district. The domestic advances for other day-workers had been intended to remove anomalies, while the increase at the other factory had merely narrowed the previous substantial differential between the two plants. To concede the present claim would create new anomalies. The company asked however for an adjournment of the conference to allow further domestic discussions. This was agreed; but the talks proved unsuccessful, and the union registered a retrospective failure to agree.[2]

Local. When the union repeated its arguments at this level, the company offered an advance of 6d. an hour, with the promise of a further review of cleaners' pay after six months. This the union agreed to recommend to its members.

This was one of a number of cases in which management failed to respond materially to the union claim at Works Conference, but offered a considerable concession at Local

Conference. The proposal to adjourn the Works Conference did however indicate some willingness to reach a compromise at that stage. Management attributed its handling of the reference to a desire to rationalize its pay structure and prevent competitive leap-frogging between its two factories. By delaying settlement until Local Conference the company could formally record 'on the notes' its intention to review the pay of cleaners at both factories so that conditions might be standardized. As with a number of pay claims resolved at this level, the workers concerned did not suffer financially from the delay since their advance was backdated.

2. 'To claim a substantial wage increase for members employed in the Factory Tools Stores Department'

This reference concerned a group of skilled craftsmen and a small number of semi-skilled workers who were responsible for the manufacture and servicing of jigs, tools and fixtures. The company had recently negotiated a revision of its payment structure based on a small number of grades. This group of workers contested the pay grade to which it was assigned.

Works. The union based its claim on grounds of comparability: the skilled men were involved in a considerable amount of toolroom work yet received some £2 less than analogous workers in other departments; while the semi-skilled workers were paid some £3 less than semi-skilled production operatives. The company accepted the validity of these comparisons and conceded the claim.

The reference was one which might well have been resolved domestically. However, the pay structure changes were involving the company's Personnel Department in an unusually heavy workload, and the tool-stores workers were pressing for quick results. By obtaining a Works Conference the union was able to achieve a speedy settlement.

3. 'To claim a substantial wage increase for our members employed in the Research and Development Department'

This claim was on behalf of five craftsmen employed on staff conditions who had recently been organized by a manual trade union. Some three months before the Works Conference the union's convenor had approached management for recognition of his right to represent these members and to claim increased pay. The company, after seeking the advice of the Employers' Association, conceded recognition; but it pointed out that it was currently reviewing the pay of this group of workers. Shortly afterwards, the company announced significant increases. Subsequently the convenor made a formal approach to management, welcoming the increases but claiming a further advance. After failure to agree, the reference entered external procedure.

Works. The union argued that it was an established custom of the district for pay for this type of work to be related to the average earnings of skilled production workers. On this basis, its members were substantially underpaid. The company replied that it was already aware that a problem existed, and had applied considerable increases. It was prepared to offer an additional £1 to take effect immediately; a merit review after four months; and a revision of age scales so that the full rate (currently applied at 25) might be paid earlier. The union accepted this as an interim settlement 'but retained the right to go back to the company should sufficient progress not be made during the year'.

This case was a fairly simple one of a previously unorganized group of employees whose conditions were significantly less favourable than those prevailing in the district. In procedure, it was doubtless possible for the Employers' Association to impress on the company the need to bring itself rapidly into line. The warning which the union attached to its acceptance must have underlined this point.

4. 'To claim an increase in pay for the Despatch Workers'

This reference, like the one which follows, involved a wage claim for a section of day-workers. The company had just completed a general review of time-workers' wages, designed to eliminate the many anomalies which had developed over the years. Management had reached agreement in principle with the convenors on the advances to be applied to each section; but in two areas the workers themselves insisted on far larger increases than were offered. Management agreed with the convenors that both sectional disputes should go through procedure, while the agreed increases should be paid in all other daywork areas. This first reference concerned a section of workers involved in the despatch of finished products.

Works. The union pointed out that while this section had been offered an increase of only 6d. an hour, other groups performing similar duties had received 1s. 6d. The despatch workers should be treated no less favourably. The company replied that despatch workers had previously earned substantially more than the other groups cited by the union. Since the whole purpose of the review had been to eliminate anomalous differentials, some sections had inevitably received more than others. The company would therefore consider only a marginal increase on its domestic offer; this was unacceptable to the union.

Local. The proceedings at this level were remarkably short. After the union's statement of case and the usual adjournment, the company conceded the claim in full.

For the union official handling the case, the company's behaviour appeared perverse. Management's view was that domestic factors (of which the union official was probably unaware) made it necessary to 'go through the motions' at Works Conference before conceding at Local. Until recently the despatch workers had been paid by results, and they were resisting any formalization of their present status as day-workers. Management feared that the section, after gaining its demands from the day-work review, might press for a return to piece-work and raise its earnings still further. In delaying settlement until Local Conference, the company was able to register formally its determination to relate the increase of 1s. 6d. to the men's continued status as day-workers. It seems likely, however, that the company's handling of the case was less calculative than this may imply; had the management representative present at the Works Conference possessed the authority to concede the claim, the reference might well have been settled at that level.

5. 'To claim improvement in payment for Maintenance Tradesmen and Mates'

Works. The unions argued that the increase proposed domestically (1s. 3d. for tradesmen and 1s. for mates) was inadequate by comparison both with the advances agreed for other day-work grades, and with the earnings of maintenance workers elsewhere in the district. The men were prepared to settle for an additional 6d., and would then be willing to co-operate in a job-evaluation exercise desired by management. The company replied that all employees were already committed under an earlier agreement to co-operate in job evaluation. While district comparisons had been considered in making the domestic offer, management was prepared to concede an additional 3d. to meet this argument; this would bring the offer into line with that already accepted by other maintenance workers employed by the company. This was unacceptable to the unions.

Local. At this level the company raised the question of possible domestic repercussions if the claim were conceded; it would not countenance any claims for similar additional increases by day-work sections whose advances had already been agreed. The union officials, as representatives of all other day-work sections, gave an assurance that no such consequential claims would be forthcoming. On this basis the full demand was conceded.

The present reference appears to have caused considerable embarrassment to the unions' convenors, who had already agreed to an increase of 1s. 6d. for other maintenance workers. They may well have urged management not to concede the claim. The company itself was clearly concerned at possible repercussions of any concession; as with the last reference, by delaying the settlement until Local Conference it was able to obtain a formal safeguard 'on the notes'.

6. 'To claim an increase in earnings levels—all Checkers'

For some years, this largely piece-working factory had experienced problems in regulating the pay of time-rated 'indirects'. A multi-factor bonus system, introduced during the previous year, had not ended the process of intermittent sectional claims for advances. Shortly before the present Works Conference, it was agreed that the whole day-work structure should be reviewed in a year's time. Meanwhile, interim increases were separately negotiated for each section of day-workers. The last such claim to be considered was for checkers and degreasers, whose rate of pay had traditionally been the same. At management's request the two groups of workers were separated in procedure. (The reference on behalf of the degreasers is discussed below.)

Works. The union claimed an increase of £2 10s. to raise the checkers to the level of pay just agreed for storemen, on the grounds that the duties of the two groups were analogous. The company repeated its domestic offer of an increase of £1 on the checkers' base rate, and a small addition to the bonus. After discussion it improved slightly the proposed increment to the bonus; the total value of the two-part package was thus raised to 25s. This was unacceptable to the union.

Local. The union repeated its arguments for parity with the stores, enumerating the checkers' duties and responsibilities. In informal discussion the company pointed out that, since the checkers enjoyed a higher bonus than the storemen, its previous offer would in fact produce parity of earnings, even though leaving a sizeable differential in base rates. It was finally agreed that the 25s. offered should be applied wholly to the checkers' basic rate, leaving their bonus unaltered. The differential in base rates was accordingly narrowed, though by no means closed.

7. 'To claim an increase in earnings levels—all Degreasers'

Works. The union claim, and the company offer, was exactly the same as for the checkers.

Local. The company here refused to move beyond its offer at Works Conference, and this was eventually accepted by the union.

With both references, the company's primary concern was that the advances conceded should not be out of line with those already accepted domestically by other day-work sections. It also felt that while checkers and degreasers had traditionally enjoyed the same rate of pay, the former had by far the more responsible job. By dealing with the two groups separately in procedure, the company sought to lay the basis for differential treatment at a later date. This objective was further facilitated by the differing settlements in the two references; while checkers and degreasers retained parity of earnings, their basic rates were separated. A more radical divorce—possibly at the time of the forthcoming day-work review—might well be anticipated.

The union favoured the policy of greater co-ordination of day-work pay movements; and its official recognized that the company's domestic offer to the checkers and degreasers was virtually the maximum it would concede. The references were taken to Local Conference against his advice; once there, the hardest arguments appear to have taken place during the adjournments, when together with his senior stewards he persuaded the sections' representatives to accept the company's offers.

The company's previous record perhaps encouraged the checkers and degreasers to press their claim through procedure. It had been a common complaint of trade unions that management failed to give their claims serious consideration domestically or even at Works Conferences; it was necessary to go at least to Local to achieve realistic negotiations. The company appeared to have tacitly accepted that there was some substance to these charges, for its personnel function had recently been re-organized; management now declared its resolve to give a realistic and considered response to claims domestically, and then stand firm through procedure (unless cogent arguments for concessions were put forward by the Employers' panel). This new style of negotiation was apparent in these two references; but it would be surprising if workers on the shop floor immediately appreciated the change.

8. 'That the indirect loaders' job be reclassified'

This reference was a claim for the regrading of a gang of nine men (which would have involved an increase in weekly wages of about £3 each). The men's jobs involved the identification of different types of component according to a colour marking system; their selective storage; and the subsequent loading of each type as required onto a moving line. The company had offered domestically to upgrade two men, who would then be solely responsible for identification duties; this was rejected by the gang and a strike took place. The men were persuaded to return to work on the understanding that their claim would be rapidly processed through procedure.

Works. The union argued that the identification of components was a complex and highly responsible job. The offer made domestically implied acceptance of this contention; but since the whole gang was involved in selection duties, it would be unreasonable to upgrade only two. The company replied that the identification duties were relatively simple, and had not changed substantially since the loaders had first been allocated to their present grade. The domestic offer was not an admission that the claim was justifiable but an attempt to find some form of compromise.

Local. The union again stressed the complexity of the men's identification duties, and also emphasized the pace of work required. Turning to the company's previous reply, it argued that the job had changed substantially since the grading scheme was introduced, and that the original grading had in any case been wrong. Since management might fear the possibility of analogous claims from other groups of component leaders, the union would be willing to agree some new terminology to indicate the special functions of this gang. The company repeated its previous arguments, and insisted that it would not contemplate regrading the whole gang; but it hinted that if the union relaxed its commitment to this objective, the company might improve its domestic offer. The union still refused to accept any differentiation between members of the gang.

Central. The outcome was again failure to agree.

Following the exhaustion of procedure the gang again stopped work. The next day an informal Wages Conference was held, at which the company eventually offered to upgrade five of the nine jobs and to allow the gang to allocate these among its members on a rota basis. After a lengthy adjournment, culminating in a secret ballot of the men concerned, this was reluctantly accepted.

This reference may be interpreted as a three-way conflict which procedure proved unable to resolve. The company's position was ambivalent: it was committed to defending its grading structure and feared the repercussions of any concession to sectional militancy. At the same time it recognized that the pay structure was itself as much a product of bargaining pressure as of 'scientific' evaluation, and appreciated that the loading gang felt convinced of the justice of its claim. Management saw the compromise eventually agreed as the only realistic outcome, and suggested that it would have been happy to settle on this basis from the start. The union appreciated the company's concern about possible repercussions, and for this reason argued the case primarily on the grounds of the special nature of the gang's responsibilities. To some extent it hoped that procedural discussions might allow the company some face-saving formula for conceding the regrading. The workers themselves appear to have accepted this strategy with reluctance, feeling that the physical effort common to all loading jobs—rather than the identification task peculiar to their own function—was sufficient justification for a higher grade. For this reason they were unwilling to accept a compromise settlement; and it was this unwillingness which made agreement impossible, given management's position, until procedure was exhausted and a strike in progress. Even at this stage, only a narrow majority of the gang voted to accept the company's offer.

Against this background, there might be some doubt whether the agreement reached in fact resolved the dispute. The Union did not abandon its commitment to the regrading of the whole gang as a long-term objective. The claim was indeed revived, on slightly different grounds, soon afterwards, and while not pursued at this time beyond domestic level, the possibility remained open. There seemed to be some feeling within the Union that the compromise settlement was so anomalous and would create such problems that the company would eventually prove happy to concede.

9. 'To discuss (a) staggered holidays; (b) upgrading of male production operatives; (c) average earnings payment for waiting time'

This claim was raised on behalf of male and female employees in one department of a large factory. The central demand—skilled grading for male production workers—would have involved an increase of about 30s. a week.

Works. The union's arguments on each of its three demands were as follows:

(a) Staggered holidays were an increasingly common and socially desirable practice, and had already been introduced in certain sections of the factory.

(b) The work performed by male production operatives was of a complexity which would attract skilled grading at most other local firms.

(c) Piece-workers in this department suffered a serious loss of earnings through excessive waiting time. It was management's responsibility to ensure an adequate flow of work, and average earnings should therefore be paid.

The company made the following points in reply:

(a) Staggered holidays had been introduced at this factory only in certain off-production areas and on an experimental basis. Problems had resulted and the practice would not be extended.

(b) The company was reluctant to concede sectional claims for regrading, since further claims were stimulated in other areas of the factory. Moreover, the earnings of this specific section were already higher than the formal grading might imply. The company suggested that the union might discuss with it a revision of grading on a plant-wide basis.

(c) The guaranteed payment for waiting time was already higher than at most firms and could not be increased.

The union registered failure to agree on points (a) and (c) and agreed to an adjournment of point (b) so that management might formulate proposals with regard to job ranking.

Local. The union dropped its demands on holidays and waiting time; since domestic discussions of job ranking had proved abortive it was pursuing the grading reference. Upgrading was justified by the skill requirement of the job, evidenced by the length of time required for operatives to become fully conversant with the complexities of all their tasks. The company contested this interpretation of skill requirements, repeated its fears that sectional concessions would have wider repercussions, and urged the union to continue discussions of job grading at factory level. The union was doubtful that such discussions would yield concrete results, and registered failure to agree.

No Central Conference was requested, and the reference thus appeared to 'die a natural death'. Presumably the section of workers concerned were convinced by the Local Conference proceedings that no concession would be forthcoming.

10. 'To claim a regarding to semi-skilled grade I'

This claim related to a section of production workers at a medium-sized factory. The reference was complicated by the fact that the union had recently agreed to exploratory joint discussions of job evaluation. An 'appreciation course' for management and shop steward representatives was arranged for the week following the Works Conference.

Works. The union's arguments were brief and to the point: the men concerned had long felt aggrieved at their position in the pay structure: their aptitudes and responsibilities justified the highest semi-skilled grade. The company did not contest the substance of the claim, but stressed its desire to end the traditional process of piecemeal sectional bargaining. To proceed with the present reference would be to cut across the comprehensive review of the factory pay structure which was to be carried out jointly. The claim should therefore lie in abeyance while discussions on job evaluation took place. The union insisted that the delay inherent in the company's proposal was unacceptable; tempers in the section concerned were such that an immediate settlement was essential. Since the men's grievance could only be pursued at present through existing procedural channels, it would be necessary to register a failure to agree; if rapid progress were made with job evaluation the reference could however be dropped.

Local. The union repeated its case for regrading in greater detail; subsequent discussion again centred on the implications for the introduction of job evaluation. The company asked what would happen if the section were regraded, and the job evaluation subsequently showed such upgrading to be wrong. The union replied that it was not as yet committed to the acceptance of job evaluation; if a scheme were agreed and showed this section to have been wrongly regraded, the position would be no different than for any other wrongly graded group. After several acrimonious exchanges an adjournment took place; during informal contacts between the two sides it was then agreed that the regrading should take place on condition that the section would be down-graded if this were agreed to be necessary when the job had been evaluated.

The difficulty underlying this reference was management's fear that any concession to the claim—which it accepted, tacitly, as completely justified—would create a band-wagon effect, with other sections pressing for regrading before the introduction of job evaluation. The union for its part recognized that to negotiate an evaluation scheme (and to win shop floor approval) would be a protracted process; it was determined that its willingness to co-operate in this exercise should not cost its members their right to press reasonable claims through the existing channels. Procedural discussions did eventually provide a formula to meet the requirements of both sides.

11. 'To discuss the setting allowance on piece-work prices'

A number of piece-work problems had arisen at this firm in previous years, several involving procedural discussions. About six months before the present reference, a Local Conference had resulted in the payment of a special interim bonus while the company examined possible reforms of its piece-work structure.

Works. The unions asked first for information on the progress of the company's studies; then raised a specific problem relating to setting. A small fixed percentage setting allowance was included in all piece-work prices; but while some operators did no setting of their own machines, others might be involved in a considerable amount of setting (particularly on short runs). To meet this anomaly, an excess setting allowance was payable at the foreman's discretion; the unions asked that the level of this allowance should be raised to average piece-work earnings. On the first point, the company mentioned certain minor improvements that had been introduced, and suggested that a number of other problems arose because the operators themselves failed to observe proper procedures. A comprehensive revision of the piece-work system had been delayed by difficulties in appointing a new Industrial Relations Manager; these had only just been overcome. As a further interim measure the company offered to consolidate certain lieu payments into the basic rate, allowing enhanced piece-work earnings; this was agreed. On the question of the setting allowance, the company requested an adjournment for further consideration.

On resumption a fortnight later, the company argued that with the concessions already agreed the level of piece-work earnings in the section was now satisfactory. The unions however emphasized that adverse conditions still affected operators obliged to perform a considerable amount of setting. After informal discussion a compromise settlement was reached, providing for a small increase in the excess setting allowance.

12. 'To claim (a) increase in all bonus values; (b) change in bonus base rate'

This was a joint reference covering production workers in the finishing shop of a large factory. When payment by results was introduced five years previously in this area of the factory, a higher conversion rate had been agreed than that applying in other departments. More recently, conversion factors in other areas had been increased substantially.

Works. The unions stated that the original high conversion figure in the finishing shop had been agreed to compensate for unpleasant conditions of work. Since bonus values elsewhere in the factory had been increased, a similar increase should be applied here to restore the previous differential. Present earnings were admittedly high, but this reflected a high level of effort and productivity consequent on reductions in manning in the department. On the second part of the reference, the unions argued that the nature of the work in the finishing shop justified an increase in basic rate to the highest semi-skilled grade in the company's payment structure. The company replied that, whatever reason may have been given at the time, the original high conversion rate in the department was an anomaly conceded only to ensure the workers' acceptance of the introduction of payment by results. The present level of earnings showed that bonus values remained generous and that no increase was justified at this time. On the second part of the claim, the company did not accept that the nature of the work justified regrading.

Local and Central. In pursuing the reference the unions withdrew the second part, as a 'gesture' to facilitate settlement (and perhaps also because they felt that this part of their case lacked real substance). This did not stimulate any readiness to compromise on the part of the management, and the result at both stages was failure to agree.

The company's refusal to offer any concession in this case—though the issue was of a type which commonly admits of some form of compromise—reflected its belief that the claim had no serious basis. Management believed that the consultants who had installed payment by results in the finishing shop had been 'taken for a ride'; there had been considerable overmanning, and when this was corrected earnings had risen rapidly. Moreover, while the conversion rate had remained unaltered, this was a largely notional figure only tenuously related to the piece-work times actually agreed. But to agree to a formal increase in this conversion factor would provide an automatic rise in all piece-work values in the shop, and would provoke similar claims in other departments.

While union officials attributed the workers' level of earnings to their high productivity, they did not seem surprised at management's treatment of the claim. Although procedure was exhausted, there were no immediate plans for industrial action. The workers in the department had voted against a stoppage, partly because another dispute within the company was already causing short-time working. But the possibility was not excluded of action at some future date should conditions prove more propitious.

13. 'To discuss piece-work prices'

Shortly before this Works Conference the company and trade union had negotiated a new piece-work agreement; times were to be assessed by work-study techniques and prices determined on the basis of conversion rates agreed for each grade of labour. Where times were disputed, a procedure was specified for re-times in the presence of management and shop steward representatives. This reference involved a disputed job time in a section of some thirty workers.

Works. The union stated that the average earnings of the section were 1s. an hour below the level prescribed in the conversion rate agreement; but while management had retimed the operation it had failed to offer an increase. The company replied that the men had not followed the agreed procedure; their steward had argued that this was a waste of time. Past records indicated that the existing job prices were capable of yielding the prescribed earnings levels; the men's present lower earnings were the result of their restriction of output, which constituted a blatant use of sanctions in breach of the agreed procedure. The conference concluded with the company expressing its readinesss to meet the workers concerned under the agreed procedure, but threatening retaliation if sanctions continued.

The conference was followed by a partial relaxation of the section's sanctions. Discussions under the procedure then took place on the shop floor and an improvement in job prices was eventually agreed.

In this reference a potentially difficult dispute was resolved by a delicate blend of firmness and flexibility. Until recently, the factory had combined a low piece-work base rate with loose job prices. The new agreement had involved a substantial increase in conversion rates but a corresponding tightening of work study. The company's intention was not to create any substantial general rise in earnings—but this was widely anticipated on the shop floor. Management appreciated the difficulties involved in an inflexible imposition of work study, where the results conflicted with the men's own conception of 'a fair day's work', and was ready in this specific dispute to offer some concession; but it was determined that the workers' demands should be processed through the established procedure. There was little difference here from the official union view: that job prices must in the last resort be mutually agreed, but that members in pursuing disputes would have to observe the procedure. The main function of the Works Conference appears to have been to impress on the shop floor representatives the strength of the company's insistence on preserving the integrity of its procedure.

14. 'Piece-workers' earnings'

This reference concerned a machine shop with some fifty workers. Sanctions had recently been applied by rate-fixers in support of a pay claim; as a result there had been delays in fixing piece-work prices and operators' earnings had suffered.

Works. The union complained that delays in assigning rate-fixers to unpriced jobs were seriously affecting piece-workers' earnings. It was management's responsibility to ensure that there were enough rate-fixers to meet the demand for their services, and the union asked that operators subject to delays of this nature should receive average piece-work earnings. The company blamed recent delays on the coincidence of the rate-fixers' dispute and high absenteeism through sickness; these were abnormal circumstances and the problem no longer existed. Management would be willing to investigate specific difficulties relating to time studies which the union had mentioned, but the company would not concede the claim for average piece-work earnings. The outcome was failure to agree.

The claim was not pursued further: it was agreed on both sides that more comprehensive terms of reference should be formulated, and a new Works Conference was held shortly afterwards. The union asked for an increase in the rate used to calculate payment in the case of seven specified contingencies. The Company offered concessions on all points, but in exchange asked for certain other changes in the section's piece-work system. It was eventually agreed to hold further domestic discussions on these proposals; these resulted in rapid agreement.

In this case, numerous problems relating to contingency

payments for piece-workers were brought to a head by the occurrence of exceptional delays over time studies. After the first Works Conference, the union accepted that the particular terms of reference were merely symptomatic of a more general problem and should be dropped in favour of a broader approach. The company was anxious to standardize piece-work conditions in its machine shops in order to facilitate mobility of labour, and was able to steer negotiations in this direction. The concessions achieved by the union for its part presumably contributed significantly to an increase or two shillings an hour in its members' earnings in the four months following the agreement.

15. 'To discuss the earnings of female workers'

This reference arose at a factory employing a high proportion of female labour, which was in the process of integration into a larger manufacturing group. Changes were involved in the nature of production, and various difficulties resulted with an adverse effect on earnings.

Works. The union raised four grievances:

(a) Piece-workers were suffering through management's failure to maintain an adequate flow of work.

(b) Because of this shortage of work, some girls were being paid only the nationally agreed minimum earnings level, even though a domestic agreement guaranteed piece-workers a higher rate of payment while awaiting work.

(c) Operators were obliged to accept piece-work prices agreed at other establishments within the group, even though working conditions and inspection standards might differ.

(d) Since the plant had lost its independent identity, management no longer had the authority to resolve grievances domestically, and industrial relations had deteriorated. The present situation was therefore explosive.

In the course of a protracted discussion, the company replied to each of these charges.

(a) This was a transitional period and problems were inevitable. Earnings were admittedly reduced, but no worker had been laid off, even though the factory was at present losing money.

(b) Only a small number of girls were being paid the minimum earnings level; these were all newly trained workers who had not yet commenced piece-work and were not therefore entitled to the guaranteed waiting-time payment. The delay in starting these girls on piece-work was in part due to the number of piece-work times currently being challenged on the shop floor. During discussion the company agreed to provide an improved fall-back rate for these girls until piece-work became available.

(c) It was essential that standard piece rates should apply to the same jobs at each of the company's factories; workers were however free to challenge any time where they considered working conditions at the factory to be different from those elsewhere. The company gave an assurance that inspection standards at all its factories were identical.

(d) It was untrue that domestic management was unable to bargain in good faith. Consistency of policy throughout was essential, and issues of general principle could not be settled domestically; but local management had day-to-day autonomy.

It was eventually decided to register no finding. The union would report the company's replies to its members, and certain minor differences over questions of fact would be investigated domestically.

This reference revealed important differences within the union. In the past, local shop stewards had possessed almost complete autonomy; now they were obliged to adhere to company-wide agreement and even to accept piece-rates negotiated elsewhere. Discontent at this loss of independence was accentuated by the simultaneous shortage of work and fall in earnings. The full-time official had to advise that little could be done about this latter grievance;

the union's bargaining position was obviously weak. Since he endorsed the policy of uniform conditions throughout the company, he also refused to support the stewards' aspirations for continued independence. It appears that the union official had been given to understand that a considerable number of workers were in receipt only of the minimum earnings level; doubtless he was less than delighted to be shown to be misinformed. A large part of the conference was therefore spent in protracted adjournments during which the official argued with his stewards. The latter seem eventually to have accepted his advice that the reference should be pursued no further, and it was subsequently reported that the factory's short-term difficulties had subsided.

16. 'Ratio of savings payable under the Productivity Scheme'

A productivity agreement had been negotiated on behalf of a section of maintenance workers two years before this reference arose. One objective was to reduce the amount of overtime being worked, through the introduction of a group bonus scheme; savings in labour costs were to be divided equally between company and workers. The average cost of overtime working (basic rate plus overtime premia) was assessed as 16s. an hour; each worker therefore received a bonus of 8s. for each hour by which the gang's average overtime fell below that prevailing before the agreement. A year later the scheme was revised. In exchange for additional productivity concessions, and the consolidation of certain traditional allowances, the bonus was fixed at a higher level (about 60 per cent of savings).

Works. The union called attention to recent national agreements affecting time rates and overtime premia. The wages payable for overtime had increased, and the proportion of savings received as bonus had accordingly fallen. The claim was for the 60 per cent ratio to be restored. The company reply was that the principle that the bonus should represent a fixed percentage of savings had been abandoned with the negotiation of the revised agreement. The workers remained in a better position than under the original agreement, since the bonus still represented well over 50 per cent of the savings. The stewards' rejoinder (because of the nature of the points at issue, shop stewards played a major part in discussions at this conference) was that the enhanced bonus provided by the revised agreement was in return for concessions which they had made. They had made clear at the time that they would seek to retain the new ratio should rates of pay subsequently increase. For that reason they were pursuing the present reference. In an adjournment, it was clear that the company representatives disagreed as to the validity of the claim and the likely impact of any concession on other groups of workers. It was agreed that the conference should stand adjourned to allow further domestic discussions; these eventually resulted in agreement that the ratio of savings used in calculating the bonus should remain unchanged, but that certain allowances used in calculating the hours actually worked by the employee group should be adjusted in their favour.

This was an issue so complex that procedural discussion was of little use in achieving a settlement. No doubt it did serve however to raise negotiation to the level of management at which an authoritative decision could be taken.

17. 'To discuss management's failure to pay average earnings while attending First Aid Courses, after promising to do so'

Six months before this Works Conference an employee had been taken ill at work and had died before reaching hospital. Considerable unrest had followed, some workers arguing that medical facilities at the factory were inadequate. Management responded by undertaking to train a specified number of employees in first aid. Evening classes were arranged, but no workers volunteered to participate. A member of management then asked the shop stewards for assistance in finding volunteers, and promised that these would receive average earnings for the time spent at the classes. Subsequently the company stated that this undertaking had been a mistake; while night-shift workers were paid average earnings, after the first week those from the day shift received only their basic time rate.

Works. The unions argued that management had given a promise to pay average earnings, and it was only on this basis that workers had agreed to enrol at the course. Whatever the reason, it was wrong for management to go back on its word. The company replied that the promise was an obvious mistake, made by one member of management without sufficient thought. Night-workers lost earnings through attending the courses and it was right that they should be fully compensated; but it was unfair that day-workers should receive the same payment while suffering no loss of earnings. The company felt that to pay day-workers their time rate was reasonable; and added that all workers who successfully completed the course would benefit thereafter by receiving a small weekly bonus. The conference was eventually adjourned on the understanding that management would consider the case sympathetically at domestic level. The issue was finally settled on the basis of a small additional payment.

The reference was one which union and Employers' Association officials alike considered should never have entered external procedure. They felt that the company had for some time suffered from the lack of adequate personnel staff and a coherent industrial relations policy; as a result, trivial issues were not resolved domestically. In a different domestic climate, the stewards might have allowed management to withdraw gracefully from its unintended commitment to pay average earnings; as it was, they were incensed at the company's unilateral renunciation of its undertaking. Entry into procedure may have helped to cool feelings, and may also have allowed the union officials to emphasize to their stewards that they were unwilling to pursue the matter further.

18. 'Holiday claim'

This claim for the payment of average earnings during holidays to production operatives arose against a background of embittered relationships at the factory. Numerous disputes had occurred concerning the company's payment-by-results system. In the past, operators had received a high fall-back rate when working on jobs for which no piece-work price had been agreed; workers therefore had little incentive to compromise on disputed prices or to expend a high level of effort on disputed jobs. The company accused workers of deliberately restricting output in order to win demands over job prices; and its attempts to discipline such workers frequently provoked stoppages. Finally the company withdrew the fall-back provisions, this change being contested through procedure to York. Subsequently a new incentive scheme was negotiated, providing for the introduction of work study and requiring operatives to work disputed jobs pending negotiations at the price offered and at 'traditional incentive level of production'. Later still a month's strike took place over the interpretation of this new agreement. The holiday claim was raised domestically immediately after the return to work.

Works. The union argued that it was wrong that holiday pay should be substantially lower than normal earnings; management had appeared to accept the principle of this contention, since in domestic discussion it had offered some improvement in return for changes in working practices. The company replied that this domestic offer was made only in the context of a proposed productivity agreement. While sympathetic to some arrangement for improved holiday pay, it could not possibly concede average earnings: it also felt that the claim should not be pursued in isolation but should form part of broader discussions of problems relating to production operatives.

Before failure to agree was registered, the Chairman called attention to 'the number of sanctions currently being applied generally' by the union's members in the factory, and in particular to a written threat to stop work for one day each week until this claim was conceded. The union official was unable to give an assurance that this threat would not be carried out: 'the members would have to decide that outside the conference room'. Subsequently he suggested informally that he might be able to prevent unconstitutional action if a quick Local Conference were arranged; this he was unable to achieve, and the Employers' Association submitted a written protest.

Local. The Chairman opened by repeating this protest against the workers' unconstitutional action. The union attributed its members' action to their impatience at management's delay in handling the reference domestically, and proceeded to repeat its argument for average earnings. The company replied that while the union had the right to pursue this claim individually through procedure, any changes which might be made in holiday pay would have to be negotiated for all employees, including members of other unions; and that the cost of improved holiday pay must be offset by increased productivity. Finally the company noted that various issues relating to production workers were to be the subject of a Composite Conference in the following week;[3] this reference might best be adjourned and the question of holiday pay discussed in that context. This suggestion was unacceptable to the union.

Central. Before the reference reached Central Conference, management issued proposals for the 'establishment' of employees with sufficient seniority. Such employees would be entitled to additional holiday pay and sickness benefits, but would lose their establishment by participating in unofficial or unconstitutional action. The central authorities agreed to retain the reference for a month to allow further domestic discussion on these proposals. At the subsequent Central Conference it was reported that the shop stewards were refusing to negotiate except on the basis of their original demand for average earnings; the union agreed to a further retention and promised to offer 'guidance' to its domestic representatives. Later still it was reported that the stewards would not consider management's proposal unless the 'penal clauses' were withdrawn. Effectively, the issue was then allowed to drop—at least for the time being.

This reference would seem to illustrate the tactical use of procedure. The holiday claim represented a genuine grievance which had been raised domestically before; several months previously agreement had been reached in certain sections of the factory for a holiday bonus in return for productivity concessions, along the lines proposed by management in this case. But it appears that the reference entered procedure when it did as part of a strategy to exert maximum union pressure while negotiations took place on the piece-work agreement. Once the latter dispute was resolved at the Composite Conference—on terms which permitted a substantial increase in piece-work earnings—the impetus behind the claim was dissipated.

19. 'To discuss the manning of fork-lift trucks'

This reference concerned one 'handicapped' fork-lift truck located in the firm's stores and intended for use by the storeman to lift heavy items. All other trucks in the factory were part of a transport pool; the drivers had been incensed to discover that the stores truck had been operating (allegedly outside the stores area) when they were involved in a short stoppage.

Works. The union stressed the emotional feelings which this incident had provoked. The drivers were also anxious about possible rationalizations of the company's internal transport which might create redundancies. For both reasons, they asked for the use of the stores truck to be restricted to members of the pool. The company accepted that emotions had been roused, but asked for the reference to be considered dispassionately. It had been custom and practice for sixteen years for this truck to be used by the storeman; it would be impracticable to assign a full-time driver to the stores, since the truck was only required occasionally, while to fetch a driver from the pool each time it was needed would involve unacceptable difficulties and delays. In the course of discussion, the shop stewards insisted that the truck was used considerably more than management had suggested, and that the storeman carried out work which was definitely within the jurisdiction of the transport pool. (It was indicative of the emotional atmosphere that shop stewards took an extremely active part in discussion at this conference.) The company replied that if the storeman had indeed been performing pool drivers' work, this was without management's knowledge or permission; any complaints of this nature should be raised and investigated separately. The amount of time for which the truck was in use could be determined objectively by fitting a clock for a trial period.

After an adjournment, the union suggested that the grievance could be resolved if the stores truck were replaced by a hand truck. The company could not accept this: there was no spare hand truck available, and to purchase a new one would be too expensive. Instead the company proposed a formula which would rigidly limit the area in which the stores truck could be used. It was agreed to adjourn the conference on this basis, to allow the objective measurement of the utilization of the truck.

When this outcome was reported back to the transport drivers, they voted by a narrow margin to stop work. They were later persuaded by the union official to return so that procedure could continue to operate, and within a few days the conference was hurriedly resumed.

Resumed Works. Both sides agreed that the drivers' strike had been an unfortunate incident. The union then argued that this had demonstrated the strength of its members' feelings that all fork-lift truck driving should be allocated to the pool. Their feelings were accentuated by recent remarks by a member of management to the effect that the pool was overmanned: this had created fears of redundancy. The company replied that it was now willing to remove the disputed truck from the stores, given an assurance by the union that the pool drivers would perform the necessary work without loss of efficiency. The rumour that redundancies were contemplated was categorically denied. On this basis the reference was settled.

A comparatively trivial dispute in this case reflected a plethora of underlying conflicts. Within the company there were signs of failure of communication and absence of diplomacy. There was evidence that first-line management had allowed the storeman to drive outside his own area, and this may well have occurred during the stoppage which preceded the reference. A manager's tactless remarks about overmanning in the transport pool did little to improve attitudes. Those members of higher management concerned in handling the reference differed in their interpretation of the causes of the dispute, but agreed in denying that the grievance lacked any justifiable basis; the issue was seen essentially as a trial of strength with a trouble-making shop steward. (Surprisingly, this 'trouble-maker' scarcely intervened in the conference discussion; his members, moreover, gave a convincing impression of a strong sense of genuine grievance.) Problems also appeared to exist on the union side. Only after the strike which followed the initial conference did the full-time official become properly aware of the fears and opinions of his members. Possibly the union's convenor was in part responsible; it would seem that he interpreted recent signs of independent action by the transport drivers as a challenge to his own authority. Apparently he had advised the drivers not to pursue the present claim, and, when they persisted, had asked management not to concede. It may be significant that only when procedural discussions were supplemented by unconstitutional action were the negotiators able to approach the reference with adequate knowledge of the situation.

20. 'To discuss the dismissal of an employee'

A fight took place between two employees prior to clocking in. One reported the incident to his foreman; both were later called to the Personnel Office and were suspended under a works rule forbidding fighting on company premises. They were subsequently dismissed, but notified that if information later showed one or other to be an innocent party his re-employment would be considered. The union to which both workers belonged contested the dismissal of one, a shop steward with twenty years service at the firm.

Works. The union argued that the evidence available suggested that this member was the injured party. It was therefore unfair that he should be dismissed, especially since management had acted more leniently in such cases in the past. The company replied that the two men had made conflicting statements and that any other evidence was circumstantial. Only if one man were found in the courts to be innocent (each worker was reported to have initiated proceedings for assault against the other) could management discriminate in his favour; otherwise the only possible course was to follow the works rule and dismiss both.

Local. The union repeated that the evidence appeared to favour the member whose dismissal it was contesting; but if management insisted on preserving its neutrality it should offer to re-employ both men. The company still replied that it could not act as judge and jury between the two men, while to re-employ both would make nonsense of the works rule.

Central. Reference to Central Conference was delayed while meetings took place between representatives of the two men (resulting in the dropping of legal proceedings). The case then proceeded, but again resulted in failure to agree.

No industrial action ensued: had there been any possibility of this, it would almost certainly have occurred *before* the case entered procedure.

The company's view of this reference was one of surprise that the union should in effect pass judgment, in the absence of adequate evidence, between its two members. Management felt that an equally plausible case could be made on behalf of either, and in the absence of a verdict in the courts insisted on remaining neutral. The union however felt that the balance of evidence, while falling short of legal standards of proof, did support the member whose case it presented; it suspected that the company might have been less uncompromising had the member not been a union activist. The most likely explanation of the company's firm stand, however, probably lay in the intergroup tensions apparently behind the original fight. Management may well have feared that to re-employ the two men would be to risk a repetition of the incident, whereas to dismiss one and not the other would be to invite even worse trouble.

21. 'Payment of lieu rates for Apprentices and Junior Workers on Day-work'

In December 1969 a national agreement prescribed increases in the rates of pay of apprentices and junior workers; but firms were permitted to absorb previous payments above the minimum into the new basic rates. One trade union raised a number of objections to the application of this agreement, arguing that it was appropriate that traditional payments above the minimum should be continued. While this was in a sense a general problem, which the union raised as such informally with Employers' Association officials, it was agreed that it should pursue specific claims on a plant-to-plant basis; in this way it was able to achieve concessions at some firms at least, whereas any demand at district level would have invited a blanket refusal. Three of these claims entered procedure during the period of the present study; a fourth reference, from a different union, also related to the same national agreement.

Works. In this first reference, the union argued that minimum rates had traditionally been geared to the least profitable members of the Employers' Federation: in this area the payment of a 'lead' rate above the minimum was standard practice. Now this payment had been absorbed, apprentices' earnings compared very unfavourably with those of young piece-workers, and the gap between the pay of the 19-year-old apprentice and the adult of 20 was too great. Under pressure from the employers, the length of apprenticeship had been reduced by a year; so it was reasonable that the lead rate formerly paid at 20 should now be given at 19. Many local firms had accepted this without trouble. The company emphasized that it was entitled to absorb the lead rate; this had been paid in the past because of the low level of the national minimum, and was no longer justified.

Local. The union repeated its argument that the full lead rate should be paid, and one year earlier than previously; but it hinted at a willingness to reach a compromise settlement. The company remained adamant, but suggested 'off the record' that it might be prepared to make some concession in domestic discussions. This was unacceptable to the union.

National. The outcome was again failure to agree.

No action was taken on the exhaustion of procedure: the union seemed resigned, for the time being, to allowing the claim to drop. It had some hope, however, of an eventual favourable settlement as part of a domestic package involving various other current claims.

22. 'To consider the implementation of the Apprentices and Junior Workers Agreement and the continuation of the lieu rate payment for Apprentices aged 18 to 21'

Works. In this reference the union argued that previous payments above the minimum had been individual merit rates rather than lieu rates, and should not therefore have been absorbed. This was denied by the Company.

Local. Discussion again centred on the status of the previous supplementary payments: whether the differential had been a discretionary merit rate or a commonly applied lieu rate. Again there was no agreement.

National. At this level the union no longer pressed this argument, and accepted that management had been entitled to absorb the payments. Instead it contended that the company should take account of general pay levels within the factory; in the interests of internal comparability the apprentices should be paid above the national minimum. The employers replied that the company was now willing to introduce a genuine merit scheme for apprentices, and would be prepared to discuss its general principles with the shop stewards. On this basis the case was referred back for domestic settlement.

With this reference, a genuine bargaining situation developed only at national level. The union agreed to drop an argument which was in some ways embarrassing to management, since it alleged that the company was in breach of agreement; the latter in turn acceded to the union's objective of an enhanced payment, but offered this in a form which would be strictly under the control of management.

23. 'To consider the implementation of the Apprentices and Junior Workers Agreement and the rate paid to Apprentices from 15 to 19 years of age—Day-workers and Piece-workers'

Works. Again the union complained at the absorption of lieu rates, and laid particular stress on the differential—over 100 per cent—between the pay of the 19-year-old apprentice and the adult rate received at the age of 20. The company replied that it had adhered strictly to the national agreement, and added that a recent domestic wage agreement had been extended to apprentices: they were thus already paid above the national minimum. The company hinted that it might be prepared domestically to consider the specific question of the rates for 19-year-old apprentices. The union registered failure to agree.

Before the date of the Local Conference, agreement was reached domestically along the lines of management's suggestion at Works. The apprentices' rate was increased by a small amount at the age of 18 and by £1 at 19.

24. 'To claim youth's percentage on piece-work prices'

This reference arose in the aftermath of the same national agreement, but concerned junior piece-workers rather than apprentices. The practice at this company was for workers aged 15 to 17 to receive a third of adult piece-work prices, and those aged 18 and 19, two-thirds. The Apprentices' Agreement had defined minimum rates as a proportion of the basic time rate for adult craftsmen, ranging from 35 per cent at the age of 15 to 75 per cent at 19. The union asked that juvenile piece-workers should now receive these percentages of adult piece-work prices.

Works. The union argued that it was unfair that juveniles should be paid less than adults for the same piece-work production. Youths on piece-work had scarcely benefited from the national agreement, since their piece-work values remained unchanged. The company replied that the national agreement related solely to minimum rates and was not intended to increase piece-work earnings. Young piece-workers still earned considerably more than time-rated apprentices, and any concession to this claim would increase the disparity even further.

Local. The union again stressed the inequity of paying youths less than adults for the same work, and indicated the size of the earnings differential between the 19- and 20-year-old piece-worker. The company repeated its previous arguments, adding that its records showed that juvenile earnings at the factory compared very favourably with others in the district and were approximately 50 per cent above the apprentices' time rate.

National. A National Conference was arranged, but the union representatives did not attend. It is possible that they considered that the case should be treated as a piece-workers' rather than a youths' reference and should go before Central Conference at York. The local official insisted, some months later, that the issue was still very much alive and would be raised again; but there was little to suggest that the national officials had not decided to let the matter drop. Failure to agree was ultimately recorded by exchange of letters almost a year after the Works and Local Conferences.

25. 'Mr A. Worker'

A year before this reference arose, Mr Worker had been formally classified in a specific grade within the firm's staff structure. Six months later the company issued a new scale of maximum and minimum salaries for each grade; employees whose salaries were below the new minima for their grades were informed that they would not be downgraded. The new minimum for Mr Worker's grade was some £200 above his current salary.

Works. The union argued that since the company had classified Mr Worker within his present grade and had since confirmed this classification, it was obliged to pay him the salary it had now defined as the minimum for this grade. The company replied that the announcement of the new salary scales was related to a restructuring of the grading system. Management had decided not to downgrade existing employees whose job had now been classified differently; but it had never been the intention that such employees should receive the minimum salary for a grade in which they were, in effect, wrongly classified. Considerable argument then centred around the interpretation of the company's letter to staff, until the Chairman suggested that the issue might be disposed of by negotiation. Eventually it was agreed to raise Mr Worker's salary by £100 and let the matter drop.

As this reference indicates, a situation can quite easily occur in which the intentions of a party in its own view are clear, but in which its actions or statements are open to very different interpretations. A compromise may well be the best way out of such an embarrassing situation, yet each side may refuse to modify a stand which it considers fully justified in principle. Even so comparatively minor a case may thus enter procedure before negotiation becomes possible. Once the reference reached this stage, the union's firmness in supporting its member (who was in any case aggrieved at the size of his award in the recent salary review) helped persuade the company to make some concessions.

26. 'A substantial salary increase'

This reference covered two dozen supervisory and other salaried staff, both monthly and weekly paid. The union submitted a claim domestically for a new salary scale, involving a narrowing of differentials and a minimum increase for all staff of £750. Subsequently the demands were reduced by £150; the increases proposed under this revised claim would have averaged just under 40 per cent. The company offered increases averaging 10 per cent, and attached four conditions: all national agreements should be honoured by the union; the increments might be withdrawn if the staff engaged in industrial action; monthly staff would be expected to undertake reasonable overtime without extra pay; and there should be no further claims for a year. This was not accepted.

Works. The union argued that the existing pay levels were inadequate. Staff required special technical competence: for this reason, appointments were made initially on a probationary basis. Monthly staff were not paid for overtime they were required to work. It was possible for manual employees, working overtime at premium rates, to earn considerably more than weekly paid staff. The company denied that staff duties were as specialized as was suggested; the probationary period was a test of general suitability rather than technical expertise. The comparison with manual employees was unrealistic; the union had taken the case of one hourly paid employee with special duties, who earned well above the average. The company had already offered substantial increases. It was unwilling either to concede a larger general advance or to agree to a further narrowing of differentials (since weekly paid staff *were* entitled to payment for overtime). After an adjournment, the union insisted that its comparison with manual ever prepared to agree to a general increase of £300, with further domestic discussions to establish new minimum earnings was valid. To facilitate a settlement it was howsalary scales. This was rejected by the company.

Domestic discussions were subsequently resumed, and an improved company offer averaging about 12 per cent was accepted by the union representatives.

This reference arose from a newly unionized group of staff, whose representatives were necessarily inexperienced in negotiating techniques. The use of procedure doubtless served to relieve these representatives of the burden of negotiation, and presumably allowed the full-time officer to advise what level of settlement might reasonably be expected.

27. 'Salary Disparities'

The union organized staff in several departments within this factory. In recent years, average salaries in one department had risen considerably above those elsewhere, which disturbed traditional relativities. The union had expressed concern domestically about this situation, and management had undertaken to deal with any anomalies in its annual review. But the increases given had increased differentials still further.

Works. The union described this background, and argued that considerable discontent had been created in the lower-paid departments by management's action. It claimed that salaries at the factory were below those at other firms in the same group, and asked that salaries in all departments be raised to the level of the highest-paid. The company replied that it considered its recent merit review a fair one: differences between departments in average earnings reflected differing lengths of service, a factor considered in awarding merit increases. While denying that any *general* anomalies existed, the company would be willing to discuss the cases of any individuals who, in the union's view, deserved further increases. Alternatively, management was prepared to carry out a job-evaluation exercise on all the union's members 'in an attempt to resolve this sort of problem for once and for all'. The union rejected both suggestions.

Local. The union reiterated its previous arguments. The company, while insisting that it still considered the salary review a fair one, admitted that the widening of differentials had created a problem. It was therefore prepared to settle the claim domestically by restoring the previous relativities, if the union would agree subsequently to discuss with management 'the relative worth of various jobs done by its members', so that the problem should not recur. After considerable informal discussion, in the course of which the union sought clarification of the company's offer and pressed successfully for the increases to be backdated, this was accepted.

This was a further example of a reference which the management, having resisted domestically and at Works Conference, conceded virtually in full at Local. Three possible explanations may be suggested. First, the union did possess a reasonable case: management had given undertakings before the salary review which were not borne out. At Works Conference the company recognized the need for some adjustment: by the next stage of procedure it may have become convinced, possibly with the advice of Employers' Association officials, that concessions were appropriate. Since the traditional policy of the company was to assess staff salaries on 'individual merit', it could not easily agree to adopt the principle of standardization. A second relevant factor was the union's ability to apply pressure domestically; it appears that (unconstitutional) sanctions were introduced after failure to agree at Works, and management may simply have surrendered. It is finally possible that the company's strategy was more calculated. The union's members would appear to have obtained considerable salary increases over a period of a few years, to a large extent through 'leapfrogging' sectional advances.

Management hoped to control this process through some form of job evaluation, and was anxious to obtain the union's agreement as the price of conceding this claim; it may have wished the case to go forward to Local Conference so that some undertaking could be formally recorded 'on the notes'. If this was management's aim, its success was limited; the formula to which the union agreed was, in the view of its official, 'deliciously vague', and involved no commitment of any substance.

28. 'Implementation of national agreement'

Salaries of the grade of staff covered by this reference were subject to an annual merit review. The union had indicated what it considered anomalies in the salary structure, and management agreed to remedy these. In the review which took effect shortly before the Works Conference, the company offered merit increases of between £50 and £100 to all staff. Since national pay negotiations were in progress, the offer was conditional on staff foregoing whatever advance was agreed nationally. These conditions were put to the union's domestic negotiating committee on the eve of the date of implementation of the merit review, and were agreed to. A few weeks later, to the surprise of both sides, the national negotiations resulted in a general increase of over £100.

The negotiating committee immediately raised this with the company: its understanding of the offset clause in the domestic agreement was that this should not cover the whole national advance, only an amount equal to the smallest increase awarded domestically (i.e. £50). Management replied that the union had agreed unambiguously to forego the whole national agreement; because of the size of this advance, the company was however willing to make an across-the-board payment of £25 to resolve the problem. This was rejected as inadequate. At this point, a mass meeting of members took place and repudiated any offset whatever, on the grounds that this part of the domestic agreement had been accepted without their knowledge or consent. The negotiating committee responded with a circular to members: since it had accepted the principle of an offset, it would resign 'as a matter of honour' if the members maintained this stand. The members backed down, and the committee continued to negotiate on the basis of its initial contention—but without agreement.

Works. The union commenced by arguing for the full national award, since the offset had never been agreed by the membership; subsequently it suggested that agreement might be possible on the terms proposed by the negotiating committee in domestic discussions. The company would not, however, move beyond its previous offer, and failure to agree was recorded. The union emphasized that it could not undertake that its members would observe procedure, since it considered the company to be in breach of the national agreement.

Sanctions were indeed applied by the union's members after this conference. Under pressure, the company relaxed its previous position, and agreement was finally reached domestically that there should be a ceiling to the offset of approximately £60.

This reference indicates the problems that can stem from a hastily conceived domestic agreement. Management, with an understaffed personnel function, had commenced the salary review belatedly and had put the offset proposal before the union representatives without allowing time for consideration of the full implications. While the company was reluctant to disregard what it considered a clear undertaking by the union, it was concerned at the effects of the dispute on its relationship with a negotiating committee generally considered far more conciliatory than either the union's full-time officer or many of the lay members. The settlement doubtless reflected both the impact of sanctions and management's desire to resolve the issue domestically —thus excluding the district official and allowing the negotiating committee to save face with its members.

29. 'Salary increase'

This reference was on behalf of a group of ten technical staff. In domestic discussions the union had claimed a general increase of £7 5s., while the company had offered £3 10s.

Works. The union argued that existing salaries did not adequately reflect the responsibility and technical complexity of its members' work. It cited salaries of other technical grades in the same factory, and also earnings of some production workers: these revealed a disparity which would not be remedied by management's domestic offer. The company replied that it had made careful comparisons with salaries for the same grade of staff elsewhere in the district, and considered its domestic offer generous and realistic. It might however be prepared to make some further marginal concession if the union were to show more realism in its demand. In informal discussion the union reduced its demand to £5 15s. while the company raised its offer to £4 15s. The differences could not be resolved and failure to agree was registered.

Shortly afterwards, agreement was reached domestically for an advance of £5 5s. The Works Conference had succeeded in narrowing the bargaining range to a point at which final compromise might in many circumstances have been achieved without great difficulty; but in the course of negotiations each side had become too firmly committed to its 'final position'. Yet the nearness of settlement no doubt encouraged the rank-and-file union members to accept a speedy compromise; while management too was doubtless keen to settle quickly, since the staff concerned had been applying a form of sanction since the initial domestic failure to agree.

30. 'To discuss earnings and hours of work—Works Police'

This large factory employed security staff round the clock; the standard working week comprised four 12-hour shifts, with a nominal 46-hour week and two hours rostered overtime. Basic rates of pay were well above the district average for this type of work, but premium rates were not payable for weekend shifts. Just under a year before the reference arose, a domestic agreement for various staff grades represented by the union had provided salary increases of just over £2 a week. District negotiations on wages and conditions of works police were in progress at the time; but it was accepted that since the firm's police participated in the domestic staff increase they would forego implementation of the district agreement. The company did, however, undertake to consider the possibility of such implementation in a year's time.

The settlement reached at district level provided for a reduction of the working week to 44 hours, and by two further stages at annual intervals to 40 hours; premium payments were specified for overtime and weekend work. After six months the union proposed domestically that the company should implement this agreement in full, but with a time lag of 7 months. The company offered to reduce the nominal working week, following 10 months behind the district; but insisted that the rostered 4 × 12-hour working week should continue, and that there should be no special premium for weekend work. A further source of contention related to the basis on which overtime payment was calculated. For obscure reasons, a notional hourly time-rate was used, derived on the assumption that the weekly salary was paid for 41 and not 46 hours. The union asked that when the working week was reduced, this 5-hour 'allowance' should continue (thus maintaining an effective bonus of over 10 per cent over and above the overtime premium). The company insisted that this was an anomaly which must be phased out.

Works. The union did not state clearly whether it was prepared to accept management's proposed timing for the reduction of the working week, but it insisted on the demand for the district premia for weekend work. The company emphasized that its own premia for ordinary overtime were better than the district agreement, that an undifferentiated 7-day week was essential to its needs, and that the level of pay received by its police was intended to compensate for the absence of weekend premia.

Local. Before the conference commenced, the union pointed out that the last stage of procedure had now been reached—since no national agreement covered the representation of security staff.[4] After the union had repeated its demand for the full implementation of the district agreement, the company pointed out that the works police had already received an improvement in conditions as part of a general increase in staff salaries negotiated since the Works Conference. In informal discussion it was established that the union might be prepared to accept some compromise on its demand for the district premia for weekend work, and that the company would be willing to meet the union half-way through some compounding of premium rates. It was agreed to adjourn for two or three weeks to allow management time for further consideration of the issue.

When the conference was resumed, the company announced that it was now willing to implement the district conditions for weekend work; while the union accepted the domestic offer for the phasing of reductions in the working week. On this basis the reference was settled.

The fundamental issue underlying this reference was a conflict of principles within as much as between the union and employers' organizations, deriving on the one hand from commitment to district uniformity and on the other from attachment to plant autonomy. Management and staff representatives alike favoured the practice of domestic negotiations covering all grades of staff, which entailed as a corollary the foregoing of some agreements at higher levels. In this case the company had indeed undertaken to examine the district agreement with a view to its implementation (though the precise terms of this promise were the subject of dispute). But it objected, first, to the haste with which the security staff pressed for implementation, feeling that they were striving for the best of both worlds. (This union official appeared tacitly to have agreed, and indeed claimed to have delayed the entry of this reference into procedure.) The company's main reason for resisting the claim was, however, its embarrassment at the *content* of the district agreement: it felt that the premia prescribed for weekend working were suitable only for the smaller employer who maintained no more than a skeleton security staff outside normal working hours. As a matter of firm policy, management had agreed that the maximum concession possible to the union's claim would be to compound the various premium rates in the district agreement into a slightly higher domestic overtime premium; the principle of undifferentiated weekend working was considered inviolable. In this instance the Employers' Association was anxious that one of its largest members should fall into line with district conditions. At Local Conference it argued strongly that it would be in the company's own long-term interests to accept the principle of weekend premia; pressure appears to have been applied subsequently at director level to ensure the reversal of management's stand.

31. 'Annual holiday arrangements'

This reference arose from a dispute over the 1969 holiday arrangements of a section of staff. During 1968 the company announced that members of staff with a minimum length of service would be entitled to four weeks' annual leave (20 working days), provided that two of these weeks were taken during the July factory shut-down; otherwise the entitlement would be only 18 days. A national agreement later prescribed a third week's holiday for manual workers, which it was decided locally would be taken in September. Staff were asked where possible to take a week of their own leave during this additional factory shut-down, but some staff had already made other arrangements. Later still, management announced an extra two days' holiday for staff, but insisted that those who were due to work during the September break should take the two days then. Certain members of staff objected to these conditions and worked throughout the September shut-down. Management declared that they had forfeited the additional holidays.

Works The union protested that management had unilaterally imposed new holiday conditions, without any form of consulation. The members concerned in the reference had been allowed to work throughout the week in question and were penalized only afterwards. The union insisted that the two days' entitlement should be restored. The company replied that its concession of the additional days was clearly conditional on accommodation with its wishes in respect of dates; staff who had worked throughout the shut-down had knowingly forfeited this extra leave. After informal discussion the company conceded that there might conceivably have been misunderstanding for which it was in part responsible, and offered an *ex gratia* payment to settle the matter. The union refused to settle for anything less than a full two days' pay.

A Local Conference was arranged, but before this could take place a settlement was reached domestically on the basis of an improved lump-sum payment.

32. 'Improved annual holidays'

This reference arose from circumstances similar to the previous case. Staff at this firm had also formerly received three weeks' annual leave, two of which were tied to the July close-down; and when the September shut-down was agreed, staff were granted a fourth week, also tied to the new break. (This condition applied not to all staff but only to grades closely associated with shop-floor processes.)

Works. The union argued that members whose holidays were tied to specific dates suffered a limitation on their freedom of choice. In this respect their situation had deteriorated: whereas in the past two-thirds of their annual entitlement was tied, the proportion was now three-quarters. Moreover, they were obliged to delay their holiday arrangements until the manual workers had determined the dates of the factory shut-down. Not all staff suffered these adverse conditions; those who did should receive compensation in the form of an additional day's holiday for each week of leave which was tied. The company denied that there had been any worsening of conditions: it had merely followed past practice in respect of holiday arrangements. It was technically necessary that certain staff should take their holiday during the factory closure; but it would be unreasonable to impose this condition on staff where no such necessity existed. Staff whose holidays were tied were in no worse a position than manual workers, and participated with them in the ballot to decide holiday dates. While the company considered its holiday provisions already generous, it asked for an adjournment in order to consider the union's arguments.

Several weeks later management replied that it was unwilling to make any concession, and the union subsequently registered failure to agree.

Local and Central. Neither side altered its position, and the outcome at the higher stages of procedure was again failure to agree.

While this reference concerned a single company, the union's claim involved an issue of general application. It seems likely that it was pursued through procedure as a gesture of union aspiration rather than as a result of a serious sense of grievance among members at the company. This was certainly the opinion of management, and the lack of urgency with which the reference was pressed tends to support this interpretation.

33. 'Redundancy'

This reference concerned a small group of staff at a subsidiary plant a short distance from the firm's main works. It was known that the local authority intended eventually to make the plant the subject of a compulsory purchase order for development; but no action had yet been commenced, and it might have been some years before closure was necessary.

Works. The union referred to the threat of closure, and stated its view that all members at the plant should be guaranteed eventual absorption into the staff at the main works. It understood that members of management had indeed promised that this would be the company's policy; but recently a union member had been informed that because of a fall in demand he must either compete for a vacancy at another company plant some distance away, or else accept redundancy. This the union considered a breach of management's no-redundancy pledge. The company replied that no member of management had ever given an absolute guarantee of continued employment: there would be an attempt in the event of the plant's closure to transfer staff to the main works, but market conditions might prevent this. There was in any case no immediate prospect of closure. The company could do no more than note the union's remarks.

Local. The union reiterated its arguments, and listed names of members who, it claimed, had been given specific undertakings on engagement relating to their continued employment after the plant's closure. Yet the moment that a staffing problem arose, management had tried to depart from this undertaking. The company again denied that there had been a promise in the definite terms which the union asserted: in any event, the present case would not have been covered by such an undertaking since the redundancy situation had arisen through market conditions and was in no way connected with the closure of the plant. It was impossible for any firm to give blanket guarantees against redundancy for all time, since business circumstances could not be predicted with certainty. The company would, however, state that its policy would always be to consider alternative employment before declaring a redundancy; and that in any redundancy situation the union would be given advance warning and offered facilities for consultation. The union insisted that a categorical guarantee had been given, from which the company was now attempting to extricate itself; in the circumstances it could only register failure to agree.

Subsequently the Employers' Association made an informal approach to the union official, suggesting that the company, while refusing to give an absolute no-redundancy guarantee, had tried to give the firmest possible commitment to meet the union's wishes. When the shorthand notes were available both sides might consider whether any elaboration of these assurances might be possible. Later an informal conference was held at which the company announced that those staff who so wished might transfer at once to the main works; it must then be understood by those who remained and any subsequent recruits that while attempts would be made in the event of closure to provide alternative employment, this could not be guaranteed. Should redundancy be necessary the union would, however, be fully consulted. It was agreed that the reference might be adjourned on this basis, and that the understanding would be formalized in an exchange of letters between the union and the Employers' Association.

This reference was exacerbated by a critical dispute of fact. The union's members were convinced that they had been given an assurance in terms which the manager concerned denied. The company insisted that it could not in any case be committed by one member of management to a pledge which might be impossible to honour. Because of the emotions which this conflict engendered, the union refused at Works and Local Conferences to consider any alternative formulation which might achieve the objective of safeguarding its members' security of employment. Only when tempers had cooled, and it was obvious that management was determined to withhold the absolute guarantee which the union desired, was serious negotiation possible. Perhaps in part because of the possibility that the staff concerned might take industrial action (as they had, successfully, in a previous dispute), the union was able to achieve a settlement which in effect conceded the substance though not the letter of its demands. At the same time, the solution appears to have been along lines previously contemplated by management; had relationships been more amicable, the company might well have raised the possibility informally with the union at an earlier stage in procedure.

REFERENCES

1. Because of the importance in Coventry of the motor industry, the seasonal incidence of new models and variations in demand within the industry may have a discernible impact on the local distribution of issues in procedure (this is discussed below). The relative importance of wage and non-wage issues does appear to vary seasonally, though there are even larger—and apparently random—monthly fluctuations. It might be thought that the incidence of holiday references would fluctuate seasonally; in fact there is no evidence of this.
2. The retrospective failure to agree is a common device: conferences are often adjourned on the understanding that if informal discussions fail to achieve any settlement, the reference can be referred to the next stage of procedure without a resumption of the conference.
3. A Composite Conference is a rare arrangement combining features of Works, Local and Central Conferences; it is held at the works, is attended by national and local Union and Employers' officials as well as domestic management and shop stewards, and is formally recorded. This specific Composite Conference arose out of the disputed incentive scheme, mentioned above. An employer's reference asserting the company's interpretation of the scheme had gone through procedure to York; the central authorities agreed to hold a Composite Conference so that national officials and domestic representatives might attempt jointly to achieve a settlement. The conference did result, after extremely protracted discussion, in a revision of the incentive scheme; but it was agreed not to discuss the holiday issue in this context.
4. It was the practice of the district for normal procedure to cover this grade of staff. Nationally, informal Central Conferences were commonly held; but there was no obligation on the union to participate in this procedure.